THE ESSENTIAL STAY- AT- HOME MOM MANUAL:

HOW TO HAVE A WONDROUS LIFE AMIDST KIDS AND CHAOS

BY SHANNON HYLAND-TASSAVA, PhD

Booktrope Editions
Seattle WA 2011

Edited by Jane Radke Slade

Cover Design by One Eye Designs

Author Photo Copyright Genevieve Tassava

Print ISBN 978-1-935961-26-0

EPUB ISBN 978-1-62015-030-6

For further information regarding permissions, please contact info@booktrope.com.

Library of Congress Control Number: 2011960912

Dedication

For Christopher, my partner in parenting and life; for my daughters Julia and Genevieve for giving me the most important job I'll ever have; for my parents for their eternal encouragement and support; and for my beloved tribe.

TABLE OF CONTENTS

INTRODUCTION

JUST BEFORE THE BIRTH of my second child, I launched a parenting blog, hoping to avoid a repeat of the isolation I experienced during my weeks and months as a first-time stay-at-home mom two years before. I needed a place to express my thoughts and feelings about at-home motherhood, and I hoped to benefit from discussion and connection with other stay-at-home moms who knew exactly what it was like to help a toddler on the potty while simultaneously nursing an infant, one-armedly, standing up—and to do this kind of thing all day, every day, with a weird mixture of joy and love tempered by a hefty dose of exhaustion, frustration, and loneliness. Luckily, I did connect with those moms, and that connection changed my mothering experience for the better. Keeping the blog helped me zero in on just what it was about full-time mothering that was so different from any other work environment I had ever been in.

I called the blog *Mama in Wonderland*, because my experience of transitioning to stay-at-home motherhood had felt like Alice's tumble down the rabbit hole: disorienting, surprising, delightful, and sometimes scary. There are some striking similarities between Alice's adventure and the adventure of stay-at-home motherhood. Consider: things kept shifting and changing for Alice. The cast of characters was compelling, but they made irrational demands of her. She was never alone, yet she felt completely alone.

Before tumbling down the rabbit hole of stay-at-home motherhood, I was a mental health professional—a clinical psychologist with a doctoral degree and many years of specialty expertise in the areas of women's health, stress management, and the intersection between behavior, mood, and well-being. My career as a psychologist has taken place in a variety of contexts, from medical settings to a large suburban school district, and finally a solo private psychotherapy practice. In my private practice, I focused on helping women find balance in their lives, cope with stress and emotion and major life changes, and learn positive strategies for living as happily and healthily as possible— something I do now as a freelance writer on women's health topics and a part-time private wellness coach specializing in self-care for moms.

With all that education and experience helping other women, I should have embarked upon at-home motherhood with an ease better suited to a baby-food commercial than real life, right? You'd think that I'd have been a pro from day one at coping with postpartum mood swings, meditating away the stress of toddler tantrums, and entertaining my preschooler while effortlessly juggling the cleaning, cooking, and kindergarten carpool. Uh, no. I needed *a lot* of help. This is one workplace that could definitely use a new-employee manual.

I couldn't find that manual at the time, so I decided to write it myself, for other women adjusting to stay-at-home motherhood. *The Essential Stay-at-Home Mom Manual: How to Have a Wondrous Life Amidst Kids and Chaos* is a survival guide for any woman transitioning from full-time work to at-home motherhood. I tackle the larger emotional and spiritual issues of in-the-trenches motherhood, and I detail the mundane, practical solutions for making daily mothering life easier and more enjoyable. *The Essential Stay-at-Home Mom Manual* is designed to be your one-stop shop for at-home mama self-care—the book you can grab whether what you need at the moment is advice about improving your mood or ideas for distracting the baby long enough for you to get dinner started. You'll hear from the doctor in me and the mama-next-door in me—often in the same sentence.

As a psychologist specializing in women's wellness, I see well-being as the sum total of multiple things working together: pride and fulfillment in daily work; physical health and fitness; adequate sleep; good nutrition; emotionally sustaining relationships; the successful management of emotional ups and downs; appreciation for life's blessings and simple pleasures; self-acceptance and self-forgiveness of our flaws. I've organized *The Essential Stay-at-Home Mom Manual* with these components in mind, including chapters devoted to those areas of wellness with which at-home moms often struggle, starting at the very beginning with adjustment to stay-at-home motherhood, in Chapter 1.

From there, the chapters are largely self-contained sources of guidance about one particular topic, with the exceptions of Chapters 2 and 3, which work together as an introduction to and a precise action plan, respectively, for women's basic self-care. This means that should one chapter not apply to you, you can easily skip it and go on to another. On the other hand, the book also functions well as a start-to-finish consecutive read; you never know what chapter may surprise you with a new way for you to approach an old issue. It's peppered with stories from my own mothering life and my *Mama in Wonderland* blog—not prettied-up for re-publication, as you'll see!—along with stories from women in my tribe, fellow mom friends navigating the journey through motherhood alongside me.

Because I know from experience how important it is to not only attend to your psychological and physical health but also to have a go-to arsenal of kid activities for those days that seem one hundred hours long and during which your sanity is hanging by a thread, I have included a bonus chapter that includes a handy reference list of simple, at-home, tried-and-tested ideas for keeping your children busy and entertained, without spending a lot of money or raiding a craft store.

Think of this book as a handbook for fully enjoying and appreciating the wonderful experience of being home with your children, for making the tough parts easier and the fun parts even more fun. Most importantly, though, this book is a guide for taking care of yourself while you're taking care of your children, so that one day you'll look back at your stay-at-home mom time and know that, because you were happy, healthy, and resilient, you were able to squeeze every drop of joy and appreciation out of those months or years.

It won't always be a wonderland, but it will be important, rewarding work—and some of the most fun you've ever had on the job.

ONE

From Conference Room to Playroom:

Adjusting to Stay-at-Home Motherhood

HERE YOU ARE: A STAY-AT-HOME MOM, whether with a newborn or a gaggle of school-agers, inexperienced in mothering or seasoned pro, brand-new to at-home parenting or back again after a return to work. Whichever description fits you, you're facing challenges you probably never imagined before having children. The truth is, adjustment to stay-at-home motherhood can be really hard. It's not always (or ever?) discussed at playgroups or Mommy-and-Me classes, but most women struggle to find their footing upon becoming full- time at-home mothers.

One woman plans ahead of time that she will stay home long-term with her children. Another plans to be home with her new baby temporarily, either through extended maternity leave or with some other time goal in mind for a return to work. Still another's time at home may have been unplanned, but is happening now due to unexpected circumstances such as a layoff, incompatibility between her job and the demands of parenthood, or perhaps due to medical/postpartum complications (either hers or baby's) that require her to stop working. No matter the path to stay-at-home motherhood, all of these mamas will have to adjust to a new reality.

So, How's the New Job?

A woman's challenges adjusting to her new role as an at-home mom vary depending on the route she took to at-home mom-hood. Obviously, being home full time with a new baby, or older children, will feel different if you and your family have planned for it over several months than if you've suddenly been thrust into a situation you feel ambivalent about or even fearful of. Similarly, you may face your new lifestyle differently if you know you'll be returning to work in a set time period rather than spending the foreseeable years at home. But some commonalities definitely exist, and we're going to talk about how to adjust to this new job—a job unlike any you've ever had.

The first step in adjusting to stay-at-home motherhood is to understand that all the challenges we'll talk about are real, and that your "*What the heck?*" reaction is valid. It's *normal* to feel frustrated that at-home motherhood is the only job around that requires 24/7 shifts and includes lunch "breaks" during which you feed, in addition to yourself, another human being. It's normal to miss coffee breaks with your colleagues every afternoon at three. It's perfectly normal to wonder how in the world you could be so intelligent and talented in so many ways and yet not have the slightest idea how to handle a crying baby.

And even more than normal, it's *okay*. Because once you understand that no, you're not overreacting to this stressful new gig and no, you're not selfish to crave some kudos now and then for how hard you're trying, you can go about the business of conquering these challenges in adjustment to stay-at-home motherhood.

Here are some of the main challenges faced by new at-home moms, and a fresh perspective on each:

☐ *Lack of knowledge and expertise in your new position.*

While this one will be most striking for new moms, let's face it: it can be crazy-making to go from a career in which we generally feel competent, capable, confident, and maybe even expert, to a new job for which we've had either no training at all or the minimal amount of preparation offered by books we read and classes we took during pregnancy. And, did you notice, those books and classes that were so compelling as childbirth loomed ever nearer hardly mentioned what to do *after* the baby arrives?

Parenting a baby is hard. Parenting a newborn is shockingly hard. And most of us didn't get a graduate degree or complete an experiential internship in Being a Full-Time, Stay-at-Home Mom. It can be more than a little disorienting to suddenly be the CEO (Oh, and hey! Also the middle manager, administrative assistant, and custodial staff!) of Project "Baby/Toddler/Child-Raising," when you either missed the new-staff orientation because you were busy with third-trimester manic Twizzler-eating or you slept right through it.

☑ *Not an expert? Not a problem!*

The thing about not being super-knowledgeable about this whole new-baby, at-home-motherhood thing is that no one else is either—not at first, anyway. Or, at least, not very many people are, and despite what you may believe in your own understandably insecure mind right now, it's not likely that you're going to run into any super-expert newly-at-home moms of new babies on a regular basis. Even the ones who seem calm, collected, and naturally suited to handle every infant crisis are most likely struggling behind closed doors.

I am reminded of my dear friend Kristi, who after the birth of her first baby seemed, from afar, to be having a remarkably easy time of it, cruising the seas of new-motherhood like she'd been doing it for years. Since my own experience with first-baby new-motherhood a few years before had bordered on the hysterical, I was amazed at how well she was doing, and told her so. To which she responded, "If doing well means standing in the basement naked to my waist, sobbing about the fact that my only remaining clean nursing bra is not yet dry from the wash and clearly this means the world is ending, then yes, I'm doing well."

See what I mean? Most new stay-at-home moms are just like you: floundering, confused, disoriented, and exhausted from finding out all the things they don't know. *Which is exactly why you need to connect with them.*

The best antidote to feeling like a floundering idiot for the first time since middle school cheerleading tryouts is to find other floundering idiots with whom to commiserate and cry and laugh about all of your floundering idiocy. Why do you think new-moms' groups are so popular?

Truly, sharing the frustrations of this tough new job with other women going through exactly the same thing is balm for the soul. Think of it as new-employee training, or professional networking happy hour. Find yourself a group of fellow new at-home moms, and talk. Do this on a regular basis, once a week at least. Do this in as many forms as you can: an informal weekly morning moms' coffee among friends, a weekly professionally-led moms' support or education group through a hospital or local community services department, a just-for-fun baby music class. You'll walk away lighter.

Oh, and in this age of social media connection, don't forget the thousands of blogs and online forums written and populated by your fellow moms. Sometimes someone you've never met and who lives several time zones away from you can be an invaluable source of commiseration and support.

Beyond that? Don't go overboard on the reference material, because it's really not necessary, but remember that there is information out there. If you need basic facts about things like diapering, nursing, infant growth, health concerns, and the like, consult your pediatrician, a lactation specialist, a home health nurse, a baby-care book, or a website written by a trusted professional or experienced parent who's been through all this before. When all is said and done, your primary source of information about the best way to care for your baby will be—trust me on this—you.

☐ *Loneliness and isolation.*

This is a biggie, and near-universal among the at-home moms I have known over the years. It tends to get better with time, but in the beginning months of stay-at-home motherhood—especially in our modern age of more dual-career couples and less nearby extended family for support—the notion that you have no co-workers in this new gig can hit you pretty hard.

I remember living in the city after my first daughter was born. The nearby new-mom-and-baby classes were hard to get into, leaving me alone with my infant each day, often without adult interaction between 8 a.m. and 5 p.m. It was horribly lonely, even on our best days. And that spring morning, *11 months* into parenthood, when my now-friend Rachel pushed a red stroller down the sidewalk across the street from my house, saw my daughter and me on our front steps, and yelled, out of clear desperation, "Are you a stay-at-home mom too????" it affirmed for me that I wasn't the only one pining for a co-worker in this most difficult job.

☑ *Your co-workers are everywhere.*

The good news is that when you reach out to other moms in sympathy over your mutual cluelessness in this crazy new job of yours, the loneliness problem gets taken care of at the same time. True, you may not become best friends with every mom at Baby Gym, but chances are good that you'll click hard with one or two, and those friendships will help carry you through your adjustment to stay-at-home motherhood. Some of my dearest friends today are the ones who have heard me complain about postpartum indignities, wail over near-constant nursing, and catastrophize that the baby would surely never, ever sleep through the night and I'd be forced to go away to college with her to field her overnight distress calls. I did the same for them.

Everyone needs co-workers. Your co-workers happen to work in different houses than you do. You can still compare notes, vent frustrations, ask for tips, and collaborate on particularly thorny work projects. You know, like sleep training the baby.

You don't need to join a group or take a class to meet fellow at-home moms, though doing so makes the process much easier. The key is to be outgoing, maybe even a little bold, and introduce yourself to any other mom who looks friendly, a tad harried (just like you), extremely sleep-deprived (just like you), and perhaps in need of a fellow-mom friend as well. Remember my neighbor Rachel, the one who shouted in my direction from across the street? After six years, three moves, two more babies, and a divorce, we're still long-distance friends, keeping up with each other's mothering lives via Facebook—and all because Rachel is the sort of person who shouts to a total stranger from across the street. You have to be a little like that.

☐ *Lack of feedback on your work performance.*

Many of you wise mamas may recognize this right away as a benefit. Who wants to be held accountable for every unsterilized pacifier, every potential choking hazard snatched out of the baby's hands in just the nick of time, each public-outing crying fit (perhaps even yours)? I know that I've been grateful these past several years not to have each gaffe and stumble during my at-home-mom workdays witnessed, rated, and sent back to haunt me.

But even so, once again, many of us modern moms entered motherhood with years of career experience behind us and a comforting familiarity with the protocols that accompany many a professional job. Many of us liked—even lived for—those gold-star rewards of glowing performance reviews, maybe even a promotion now and then. It felt good to be told we were on the right track and that our work was appreciated.

I probably don't have to tell you that the only promotion you're going to get as a stay-at-home mom is the eventual upgrade from "constantly used as a Kleenex" to "potentially able to shower (alone) without having to open the curtain halfway through to remove a child's arm from the toilet bowl or intervene on behalf of a serious diaper emergency."

And as for performance reviews? Well, that baby isn't going to type up a memo complimenting you on your animated board-book reading or your remarkable patience during marathon nursing sessions.

☑ *No performance reviews means you're free to write your own job description.*

Listen, this one you're just going to have to suck it up and live with, or change it on your own. This used to bother me a lot. I wanted feedback, dammit! Why wasn't anyone paying attention to how hard I was working and offering to give me special job perks as a result? Where were my gold stars? And also, what about the work areas about which I felt uncertain—was anyone going to affirm or correct me about those? Did I make a good casserole or what? Did anyone else notice my allegiance to local, organic produce? How about the way I resisted the temptation of relying on PBS Kids in order to get things done around the house? (Never mind, now, about that last one, by the way.)

If you hadn't guessed, I was the honor roll, straight A, overachiever type growing up. I know: big surprise. But a lot of us, when we tackle a new challenge, do want validation that our work is on the right track. That's how we've rolled our whole lives. It's no wonder this amorphous new gig is disorienting.

I advise a total mindset-shift for this one. In psychotherapy terms, we call this *reframing*. Reframing just means thinking of, and describing to yourself, a particular situation or problem in a different way—one with positive elements. In this case, I recommend reframing:

> *I have no idea how I'm doing in this job because there's no way to measure success (other than keeping the baby alive, which seems like something pretty much anyone could do).*

as:

> *Goodness it's nice to be free of someone else's standards for how my work should be done, and also, how awesome is it that I can perform parts of my current job in my pajamas without alarming anyone and triggering some serious questions about my sanity?*

See how that works? And isn't that better?

You need to start viewing your lack of performance feedback not as confusing and upsetting but as a major perk. It means no one's looking over your shoulder as you traverse the choppy waters of novice stay-at-home motherhood. It means you can stumble and make mistakes and learn as you go, and that's fine (even expected, and what everyone else is doing as well, if you really need a point of reference).

It also means you can make modern stay-at-home motherhood look like anything you please. Are you the boho type who eschews nap schedules and prefers stroller walks with a travel mug of tea and impromptu playdates under a tree? Go for it. Do you feel best when you live by the clock, structure your days around scheduled activities, and keep a running to-do list? Great!

Even better, beyond the obvious basics of childcare such as

feeding, diapering, dressing, bathing, etc., as a stay-at-home mom you are free to design your daily agenda as suits your needs and whims. And no one's going to admonish you later for not finishing what you started if you abandon board-book-reading for a run with the baby-jogger because the rain suddenly stopped.

Freedom is one of the biggest perks of this job. It's time to consider lack of work feedback as unspoken agreement that you're totally rocking this stay-at-home mom job. And then repeat after me: I'm the one in charge, and it's awesome to be my own boss!

☐ *No endpoint to the projects.*

When you're a stay-at-home mom, you spend your days performing an awful lot of tasks that need doing again shortly after their completion. Of course, the obvious examples are the childcare-related ones: the diapering or bathroom assistance, the feeding, the bathing, the dressing, and then dressing again when outfit number one gets soiled. And then there are the auxiliary duties of housecleaning, cooking, and laundry. The dust doesn't stop materializing on the furniture after you've cleaned the living room. You don't present a PowerPoint on how to cook a healthy family dinner and then never have to think about those particular specifics again because you're moving on to a different project (lunch?).

There isn't a time when you can say, "Whew! I completed that job and now I don't have to do it again for a very long time, or at least until the next fiscal year." The work of a stay-at-home mom is a never-ending loop. You finish—if you're lucky!—doing three loads of laundry and emptying the dishwasher, and there they are: the next soiled Onesies, the sticky sippy cups.

Sometimes you just want to experience a sense of completion, even for a day, but that's not how this job works.

☑ *The tasks never end, so find your own stopping points.*

I'll admit that this one is a challenge for me, one I'm still trying to master. All moms know that running a household and raising a young family is made up of a series of repeated tasks: making meals, doing laundry, serving snacks, cleaning the house, changing diapers (for the near future anyway), wiping bottoms (ditto), running the errands, even handling the larger-world endeavors like scheduling the social calendar and the parent-teacher conferences. This wears on all moms, but I think especially on at-home moms, whose homes are their workplaces and who don't have other places in their lives to go to where projects begin and then end.

The most important remedy for the burnout you can experience when your at-home mom work stretches before you with no end in sight is to give yourself the ends you need. In other words, while the dirty dishes aren't going to stop being generated, you can pick a time at which you stop attending to them—temporarily, of course!—and take a coffee break, an evening off, or a Saturday away. You can work from the baby's waking until, say, six o'clock, at which point your spouse or partner takes over some of the household and childcare work. You can pick up toys at two set times per day—before lunch and before bedtime, for instance, and let that "project" be completed afterward, for a while—during which time you do not keep picking up toys over and over and over whenever you see some toys to pick up. You can relegate Sunday mornings to lounging with your kids in bed and snuggling, even though you're fully aware there is laundry to do.

No one else is going to give you these endpoints. Remember, you are the boss. And since the jobs themselves don't truly end, the only way you're going to get a break and a sense of completion is if you take it, and make it, yourself. So do it, because if you don't, you'll eventually get to the point where your frustration at the tedium of making lunch over and over and over again will come out in somewhat unbalanced behavior involving tears and excessive consumption of chocolate.

☐ *No paycheck.*

This one is self-explanatory, right? And it's also not a challenge you didn't know about beforehand. However, you may not have predicted how much the lack of a paycheck would bother you. I don't just mean the often-unpleasant financial realities of giving up one of your household's incomes to raise children (though this part can be extremely daunting, which is why I have devoted a chapter to it later in this book—Chapter 9: Living a One-Income Life in a Two-Income World).

I mean just the lack of compensation in general, for what often feels like a much, *much* harder job than the one you had before—that one with a paycheck every two weeks. I know that in my first year of at-home motherhood there were many times I thought wistfully of those slow afternoons at my old office, when I could easily while away an unexpected free hour surfing the Internet for *People* magazine articles on celebrities' pregnancies. I'm not saying I didn't work hard, but let's be honest, most jobs come with a fair degree of time-wasting, socializing, and coffee-break-enjoying. None of which I seemed to be doing as a postpartum full-time stay-at-home mom. I distinctly recall thinking to myself that public speaking and client meetings and grant proposals were like lying in a hammock being hand-fed M&Ms compared to a caring for a baby who would only nap in my arms after nursing and then only if I didn't breathe or sneeze.

We all know the payoff is a happy, healthy child and the fulfillment of sharing as many developmental milestones and fleeting, sweet moments with him or her as possible. But those rewards are generally years away. In the meantime, a little cash would be nice. Consider my less-than-cheerful description of a typical day in my new at-home mothering job, one of the earliest posts on my blog, *Mama in Wonderland*, started shortly after I closed my therapy office to focus solely on parenting two babies two and under:

> *I figured out yesterday that between 7:30 a.m. and 10 p.m., I had a total of 25 minutes away from the incessant needs of one or the other baby, when I went outside for a very brief workout. You know—the nursing, the toddler not napping, etc. Can you think of any other job where you work a 14-hour day with only 25 minutes of break-time? And where you have to feed two other people during lunch?*

> *And I'm not getting pay or retirement contributions for this job because....?*

Let's face it: days like that deserve overtime pay. Stay-at-home motherhood is a volunteer position, though, so you might occasionally need to remind yourself about why you volunteered in the first place.

☑ *No paycheck does not mean no value.*

I know you know this one. I know you know that just because you don't get paid for the work you do as a stay-at-home mom, it does not mean your job isn't important, valuable, and worthy of compensation. But it can still be hard to withstand the discouragement, not to mention the financial strain, of working really, really hard while making no money whatsoever.

It's not that we stay-at-home moms think that the heart-consuming job of mothering can be reduced to mere monetary compensation, or that we'd trade it for dollars and cents any day. It's just that sometimes it can be hard to value your own work, to remember your fundamental worth to the family, and to present yourself to the world as capable and valuable, when your day-to-day job does not help pay your household's bills nor fit neatly into a clichéd economic category (white-collar work? blue-collar work? middle-class? upper-class?). Let's face it: our society values money, material possessions, career achievement, and upward mobility. Where do stay-at-home moms fit into that schema?

But much like the "no performance feedback" issue, the "no paycheck" problem cries out for reframing. Since none of us is likely to experience a change in this reality anytime soon, the only thing to be done is to think about it differently. Rather than ruminating on your situation from a viewpoint of scarcity and loss, switch your thinking to consider your unpaid status as something else—something positive.

Are you economically blessed to be able to afford to stay home? Does your husband or partner have an awesome job with great benefits that can support your mothering goals? Are you struggling financially, but you know it's a temporary state that will pay off in emotional and family fulfillment for years to come? Is your worth measured in happy, healthy kids, home-cooked meals, energy, enthusiasm, friendship, volunteer work, rather than dollars and cents? Is it not ideal, but working okay for your family right now? Do you know in your heart you're worth more than the CEO of a major financial institution, no matter what your personal finances?

You can do this. You can reframe the volunteer nature of your new job as something you can live with, even appreciate. And when you do that, you'll be more able to enjoy each day for what it is: a gift to you and your children *now*, which will possibly or probably be replaced in years to come with days spent engaging in some sort of part-time, full-time, or flex-time paid work. Or maybe not, but at any rate, remind yourself that right now you really do have the most important job in the world, paid or unpaid: shaping and guiding the development of the next generation.

Remember: Adjustment is an Ongoing Process

Do you feel a little better now about the challenges of adjusting to stay-at-home motherhood? I hope so. I hope these ideas have helped you realize how very normal your difficulties and concerns about leaving the career world and entering the stay-at-home motherhood world really are. I hope this chapter has given you some new ways of looking at and thinking about the dilemmas you're facing. And more than anything, I hope you remind yourself of the points I've discussed here, and that you re-read them from time to time—any time the stresses of modern stay-at-home motherhood have you pulling out your hair.

Adjustment to stay-at-home motherhood doesn't end at three months, or six months, or when the baby turns one. It doesn't end when baby number two comes along, or when they're both out of diapers. It doesn't end at preschool, or kindergarten, or the first time they climb the steps onto the school bus. Amazingly, and sometimes infuriatingly, adjustment to at-home motherhood is ongoing, taking new forms and nuances at every novel stage of life and child development. The things you have to get used to as the mom of a newborn are different from the things you have to get used to when you send your youngest off to all-day school for the first time. The challenges of spending all day with toddlers morph into the challenges of being the kindergarten room parent, or weighing the pros and cons of taking on a new part-time job from home.

But many of the coping strategies and comforting elements discussed here in relation to the initial shock of becoming a stay-at-home mom are relevant and necessary no matter your children's (or your own!) ages and stages. Because think about it: connection with like-minded moms, friendship, empowerment, setting limits on drudgery, enjoying the moment, reframing toward the optimistic and positive, knowing your own value— aren't these eternally beneficial? Won't these things serve you well for years to come, as you coach peewee soccer or help decipher sixth-grade math homework or chaperone the middle-school dance?

Of course they will. You will adjust. You *are* adjusting, right now, every moment of every day. No one ever said it was easy (or did they? curse them!). But "easy" was never the point.

TWO

MAMA SELF-CARE:

"IF MAMA AIN'T HAPPY, AIN'T NOBODY HAPPY"

BEFORE I HAD KIDS, I used to think those anecdotes about postpartum moms not even having time to shower while taking care of their newborns were exaggerated, terribly pathetic, or both. Seriously, how long is a shower? Ten, maybe fifteen minutes? How in the world could someone not have time for one? Or not have time enough to get dressed before 2 p.m.? Or to eat lunch? Huh? All I could think at the time was, *There must be something wrong with those women.* Of course the fact that it seemed to happen to quite a lot of new moms should have tipped me off that something other than weakness of character was responsible for their unshowered, still-pajamaed state as they hobbled through their mothering days.

You probably know what's coming. I had a baby when I was thirty-three, after years of successful self-care and good grooming and the rigid maintenance of a schedule and a reputation for promptness that would make Miss Manners proud, and my mornings (let's face it, my entire days!) went all to hell. Take a shower every day? I was lucky to get my teeth brushed. Get dressed before noon? Uh, some of the time, like if my husband was around, or my mother was visiting, so that someone else could take over for a few minutes. Suddenly, my pre-baby pronouncements about time and self-care echoed in my ears and haunted me. "Oh my God, I don't even have time to take a shower," I was heard to say, exclaiming to my almost-universally childless friends, who were no doubt thinking, *Seriously? How long is a shower—ten, maybe fifteen minutes? How could someone not have time for that?* And so the cycle of life continued.

The Self-Care Conundrum: If You've Only Got 20 Minutes, Do You Take a Shower or Eat a Pint of Ben & Jerry's?

The truth, as all moms know—and especially stay-at-home moms, who don't have the "luxury" of solo lunch or coffee breaks during which to catch up on such self-care tasks as, uh, smoothing one's hair, applying a touch of makeup, or eating—having a baby is a little like being tossed unprepared into the deep end of a swimming pool. There's no time for attending to your form or perfecting your stroke; it's sink or swim, and all you can do is thrash around, focusing on the absolute immediate necessity of *keeping your head above water.* Lip gloss, showers, and doing one's hair become irrelevant, second to the pressing non-negotiables of feeding, burping, changing, dressing. You finish one cycle, and the baby cries for you to begin the loop again. You do. Again. And again. And again. Twenty-four hours a day.

When you get a few minutes to yourself, when the baby's just eaten and is swaddled in the bassinet, the span ahead isn't enough time to complete all the self-care tasks you really need to do—use the bathroom, grab a nap, bathe, dress, eat, drink—and so you choose the one or two most crucial. I'll give you a hint: bathing and getting dressed are not the most crucial.

I still remember my firstborn's excruciating pattern of nursing for 45 minutes at a time (not the 15 or 20 minutes all the books I'd read described), only to start up again 45 minutes after finishing the previous session, and doing this 24 hours a day, for weeks. I remember the dread of knowing in my gut that less than an hour between feedings (plus the diaper changes and, often, necessary outfit swaps that followed each feeding) was just not enough time to squeeze in the things I so desperately needed to do. I remember using that time to guzzle giant glasses of water and feverishly ingest as much food as possible—the frequent nursing was using up all my reserves and sucking the calories right out of me—and throw in yet more poopy-baby-clothes laundry. I remember racing the clock to make a quick phone call or microwave a frozen burrito. Most of all I remember the necessity of using at least 20 minutes of that time to run the breast pump, in order to slowly stockpile a supply of milk in my freezer for the part-time evening work I was slated to resume soon. I do not remember using those precious few minutes to take a shower.

Later on, when a second baby entered into the equation, the prospect of ever being properly groomed again seemed remote indeed, as I wrote on my blog the first week my husband returned to work after Genevieve's birth:

...The morning routine is killer. Anyone got any ideas about how I can ever bathe again? These babies--they both wake up at the same time...And you know, the morning needs are so pressing: the changing of the overnight diaper, the starved-baby nursing (yes, she thinks she's starved, even though she just nursed two hours prior), the inhaling of the breakfast. None of these things can wait. But YOU try nursing one baby and changing the other's diaper at the same time. Or washing one's face while simultaneously stripping the other's bed of oops!-leaking-diaper-soaked sheets. Invariably I end up in a sweat, trying to cram my nipple into Genevieve's enraged and screaming mouth while unsuccessfully spreading jam on Julia's toasted bagel with one hand. Or Genevieve ends up lying in the nursery crib wailing with fury while I haphazardly brush Julia's teeth and funnel a clean t-shirt over her wiggly toddler head.

By the time everyone is washed, dressed, and fed, I typically realize that I'm not actually included in "everyone," and I'm generally in dire need of a strong (decaf! right?!) iced soy latte, NPR on the radio, and some quiet quality time with the laptop. If I'm VERY lucky, I might get the first two, and probably not at the same time.

Surely I'll get better at this, right? Figure out a system and all that?

Maybe the morning rush gets easier by baby number three or four, but for me two babies in the house meant I was still tempted to yell, "Don't leave me alone here!" as my husband zipped off to work in the morning.

So, the Baby's Older; Why Is It Still So Hard?

But here's the thing. While there may be no antidote to postpartum slovenliness (and honestly, everyone's far more interested in the new baby than they are in you anyway, so don't worry about it), babies grow. The every-two-hours feedings stretch out, and the relentless needs of a newborn wane a bit. The baby naps longer, and can hang out happily confined in a bouncy seat or crib, gazing at brightly colored toys and batting at the dangly distractions overhead. This gives you a few extra minutes to attend to the basics of self-care that, not long before, you wondered if you'd ever have time for on a regular basis again. And, while most at-home moms of older children do sometimes fall prey to self-neglect (t-shirt, yoga pants, and haphazard ponytail, anyone?), once your children can safely be left to entertain themselves for a few minutes, taking care of yourself becomes much easier.

Sort of. In theory. The truth is, an awful lot of stay-at-home moms struggle with self-care, even when the babies become toddlers, and preschoolers, and grade-schoolers. Oh sure, we may be shedding our pj's every morning. Eventually there's the school bus stop, after all, or carpool, to show up for. But how many of us are consistently attending to all the needs that truly keep us healthy and happy, tidy and pulled together? What about the slightly larger self-care goals, the tasks beyond taking a shower and getting dressed in actual clothes? Shouldn't our self-care expectations grow along with our newborns? Shouldn't we all—those of us well beyond the postpartum period, that is—be rising to the occasion by now?

Whether your babies are in Mommy-and-Me or the second grade, I'll bet, if you're a stay-at-home mom, you're not at the top of your own priority list. How many of us are taking our vitamins every day? Drinking enough water? Flossing each night?

Exercising on a regular basis? Scheduling our medical and dental check-ups as religiously as we do our children's? Eating well? (No, the remainder of your toddler's Gerber Graduates Fruit Twist does not count.) Getting a good night's sleep, most if not all of the time? Including downtime, adult friend time, couple time, alone time in our schedules? In my experience, not many. I have a few theories about why we do this to ourselves.

I'll Take Care of Myself as Soon as the Day Expands to 36 Hours.

First of all, who has time? Okay, so I just told you that once your babies pass the newborn, constant-feeding, nighttime-crying phase, your schedule opens up to allow time for taking care of yourself. That is true, up to a point. Yes, you can now get dressed before noon. (Brand-new mamas: it will happen!) Yes, a quick wash-and-blow-dry or mini makeup application is probably possible. Sure, once you're nursing (or bottle-feeding) the baby four or six times a day instead of eight to twelve, you ostensibly have more time in your day, and why not use that time to prepare healthy meals, floss every day, get your hair done, give yourself a pedicure, have lunch with a friend?

Experienced stay-at-home moms are now laughing at me. Because, as most of us know, it's not that easy. The tasks of at-home motherhood are amorphous and never-ending; they expand to fill the available time, whether that's five minutes or forty-five. Whether you're changing a million (or so it seems) diapers a day or packing school lunches, nursing a baby or attending school-volunteer meetings, it all takes time, and it's too easy to fill every nonstop moment in your mothering day with the relentless needs of your children and family, at the neglect of your own physical and emotional self.

Was That Really Me, the Woman Who Used to Dress Nicely and Get Her Hair Done More Than Twice a Year?

Other factors come into play too. Motherhood, especially new motherhood, is all-consuming in a way unlike any other life transition. Not only does the landscape of your daily life change dramatically overnight, but your very *identity* makes a sudden shift. You are no longer your own first priority. You are no longer an untethered adult with the freedom to attend to your own desires, preferences, and goals—at least not at first, and maybe not for a very long time. For most women, this shift into motherhood includes some loss of their pre-baby selves—those selves that were focused on things other than *keeping another living creature alive, safe, and happy.*

It's easy to see how a mom might simply forget, for a time, to think about vitamins and nutrition and exercise and salon appointments to touch up that color. And while that's totally understandable, and even necessary, in those first hectic and exhausting postpartum weeks of new-baby life, it's detrimental if it becomes an ingrained habit, a default way of viewing one's self as a mom who cares for everyone else but herself.

I Need to Win the Lottery in Order to Afford These Highlights.

For some stay-at-home moms, myself included, there's also the issue of a tighter household budget. Supporting a family on one income isn't easy today, and for some of us, staying home full-time with our children requires substantial financial sacrifice. This can mean there's no extra cash for an occasional massage, coffee out with girlfriends, or the latest bestselling novel. If the budget contains any extra, it can be tough to justify treating yourself to highlights when there are diapers to buy or preschool tuition to pay. Believe me, I get it.

I'll Take Time for Myself When I Can Wrest the Baby Away From My Knees for More Than Five Seconds.

Lastly, there's the guilt factor. What is it about becoming a mom that causes so many of us to feel guilty about doing anything solely for ourselves? Is it our children's constant needs? The amazingly strong mother-child bond? The way our kids know just what to do and say to make us question our own plans (if those plans don't include them)? Worry that our partners won't approve of our personal time, or will resent us for taking it?

Whatever it is, it's not helpful.

Why It's More Important Than You Think.

But while I've laid out all the reasons why stay-at-home moms struggle with self-care, let's review all the reasons why it's crucial to engage in—even embrace—it.

Happy mama = happy family.

The maxim, "If Mama ain't happy, ain't nobody happy" caught on for a reason; namely, it's true. If you're an at-home mom, you're the heart of your family—the one handling, most likely, the bulk of the household's physical and emotional operations.

Your children's well-being depends, in large part, on your well-being. They look to you to learn how the day will go, whose needs are most important, how to relax, how to be happy. They pick up on your moods; they sense burnout and fatigue and guilt in addition to noticing joy and lightheartedness and contentment. You are their daily guide through feelings, growth, and life.

That is a huge honor, and a gigantic responsibility. It means that when you're not taking care of yourself, not treating yourself to healthy habits and good grooming and a somewhat balanced life, and subsequently feeling harried or discouraged or frumpy or sick or exhausted or unimportant, your children will notice it. And they just might respond with cranky moods of their own. Who needs that? Full-time mothering is hard enough as it is!

You need to be here for the long haul.

Every mother knows that once you've brought a child into your family you never think about life, death, and mortality the same way again. Suddenly, abstract concepts of the long-term future and delayed consequences take on a crystal-clear importance. Risky behaviors become much less enticing. (I know more than one person who has sworn off smoking, speeding, or helmet-less bicycling once he or she became a parent.)

The truth is, while forgoing salon appointments or neglecting your favorite hobbies won't kill you, a lot of other self-care behaviors are inextricably tied to physical—not to mention psychological—health, including good nutrition, frequent exercise, daily flossing, proper sleep, and regular dental and medical check-ups.

Your babies need you, mamas! Take care of yourself, starting now. You can run on fumes for a while, skipping workouts and missing out on sleep and eating slapdash takeout meals high in fat and sodium while you run yourself ragged running after toddlers, but in time those habits can lead to serious health consequences. Don't you want to be around for a good long time, to parent your babes into adulthood, to see them launch careers and families of their own, to enjoy grandbabies? Of course you do. So preserve your health now—by taking care of yourself. I'll show you how in the next chapter.

Show your kiddos how it's done.

When your kids look at you, they see a beloved hero, never-fail caretaker, the most important person in their lives. But if they also see a mom who sacrifices her well-being for the family 100% of the time, they learn that it's okay for moms to neglect themselves and be taken for granted. Start them off young learning that everyone, moms included, deserves (and gets) time and energy for their own pursuits, whether that be regular salon appointments, a nightly run, or monthly book club. Taking time for yourself models positive behaviors to your children, and trains them to respect you and your needs.

Be a rock star.

One of the best parts about being a stay-at-home mom is that sense of accomplishment and flow when you're truly rocking the awesome-mama role. I don't mean being perfect; I mean being on your game, whatever that means to you: handling the household crises, running the carpool, supervising the games and art projects and nature walks, doing the heavy lifting (often literally) of baby/toddler/childcare with energy and enthusiasm.

And guess what? You can't do all that if you're overtired, underfed, over-sugared, dehydrated, out of shape, or just plain burned out from never stoking your own fire. The life of a modern stay-at-home mom can be demanding. It includes tasks and circumstances that may have been foreign to most at-home mothers of previous generations: greater economic pressure; increased involvement in structured lessons, sports, and classes, hence a busier household schedule; and decreased availability of extended family to rely on for help.

The fact is, you will be better able to handle the many demands of the stay-at-home mom life if you are happy and healthy. To be a modern stay-at-home mom rock star, you've got to maintain the machine. And that means taking care of yourself, body and soul.

Self-Care Ground Rules

One step at a time.

When you feel motivated, it is tempting to tackle every better-life goal you've ever had. But few of us have the resources to tackle multiple challenges simultaneously. If you decide to become the Mama Self-Care Queen, and vow to overhaul your diet, start an exercise regimen, get more sleep, book a monthly pedicure, and begin flossing every night, you're likely to overwhelm yourself and lose your resolve when you flounder. My behavioral Action Plan, outlined in the next chapter, calls for making one change at a time and truly letting it sink in and take shape before moving on to additional self-care tasks.

Start small.

Who but a mother knows better that baby steps are easier than giant leaps? When learning to take time for and better care of yourself, it's imperative to start with reasonable goals and build on small successes. In behavioral psychology terms, this is known as "ensuring a success experience" so that you feel proud, happy, and certain that you can continue to do well. A sense of self-efficacy is crucial to behavior-change success and will take you a long way toward meeting your goals. If you set small goals that are attainable—say, going to sleep 15 minutes earlier at night—you can slowly add to them (20 minutes earlier, then a half hour earlier) until you reach the circumstance you're after (a solid eight hours of sleep each night, for example).

Set yourself up for success.

Before jumping into your plan for better self-care, think about what you need to succeed. Maybe it's a new pair of running shoes. Maybe it's a consultation with a registered dietician, or the name and number of a fellow-mom friend interested in starting a walking group with you. It may be as simple as a selection of nail polish shades and half an hour to yourself on a weekend morning to do an at-home pedicure. In my professional work with clients, I describe this tactic as proper stimulus control: arranging the controllable pieces of your environment in a way that will be most likely to elicit your desired new behavior. Get prepared before you start, and you'll avoid minor stumbling blocks that can turn into deal-breakers.

Expect obstacles, and don't let them derail you.

You will flounder and choose the less-healthy, just-get-through-this-day-in-one-piece action at times. What stay-at-home mom hasn't gulped four cups of coffee for breakfast in order to survive the day following a night of nonstop nursing (or vomiting)? The key to long-term success is to avoid abandoning your entire endeavor after one misstep. Remind yourself of all the reasons mama self-care is important—re-read that section right now if necessary—and know that you can make a different choice next time.

Oh—and don't expect it to feel easy at first.

Remember the guilt factor we talked about? Yeah, that's a tough one. But listen: if you know that putting yourself first may feel difficult in the beginning, you'll be more able to acknowledge the guilt, put it aside, and take care of yourself anyway. I learned, through trial and error, that with practice it does get easier. This is what I wrote on my blog the first time I left my babies with my husband on a Saturday afternoon and drove an hour away from my small rural college town to the nearby city for a fancy massage at an upscale day spa:

> *Today I drove up to the city to finally redeem a birthday gift-card for a massage at a fancy day spa in Uptown. A massage! An hour of utter pampering! For an overworked, overtired mama! Can you imagine my excitement? Talk about a rare treat!*
>
> *The massage was heavenly, but I kept thinking about my sick baby at home and wondering if she was okay—Genevieve has some sort of a virus with a nasty fever and is truly miserable—and I was also beset with an irrational worry that the massage therapist could read my mind and I would get scolded for not having relaxing enough thoughts.*
>
> *I can't help it; I kept trying to envision, oh, a placid lake or the sunset, and then veering off into less serene*

cognitive territory, involving thoughts of the grocery list, the school-supplies donation we are required to hand over at preschool orientation next month, my sister's recent surgery.

But really! It was relaxing!

It's true that sometimes you end up worrying about the sick baby during the birthday massage, isn't it? You try to throw a little balance into your busy life, a little personal time to temper all those moments you give away on a daily basis to the tiny children who need you so much, and that little slice of "balance" ends up feeling more elusive than you imagined it would.

But I'm thinking it gets easier with practice. So I'm planning on booking another massage before too long.

If you're like me, you might need to think of repeated massage appointments as your required homework in self-care. You can't just skip your homework, can you?

Enlist your partner's help.

I wouldn't have been able to drive to the city for that massage if my husband hadn't been willing to take over at home for a few hours. Someone's got to be on duty, so whether your self-care goal involves kid-free time to exercise in the evenings or the freedom to sleep an occasional entire night without responding to baby cries, you need to get your parenting partner on board. Hopefully this will be easy, because your partner fully appreciates the nonstop demands placed on you as a stay-at-home mom and wants you to get a break now and then. But even if you encounter some resistance—perhaps your partner is simply used to you being the on-duty, go-to parent, and is loath to rock the boat—you need to stand firm. Everyone deserves time to attend to her own needs. You don't get any of that time during normal working hours, whereas most likely your partner enjoys, at the very least, workday lunches that don't involve feeding another person. You certainly deserve some time in the evenings and on weekends, so sit down with your partner, explain how increased self-care time will benefit the entire household, and work out a plan. Remember: happy mama = happy family.

Finally, know that it doesn't have to bankrupt you.

Self-care shouldn't be synonymous with "expensive." We talked earlier about a tight budget as an obstacle to taking care of oneself, particularly for those of us who have sacrificed financial comfort to be stay-at-home moms. But I have found that some of the best sources of mama self-care are low-cost or even free: an hour to myself to read a magazine in bed, a (kid-free) trip to the library to nab the latest bestseller, water instead of more Diet Coke, an evening run. Taking care of yourself can be affordable; I'm living proof. Don't let your finances stop you from achieving your self-care goals.

Are you convinced? Are you motivated to take better care of yourself from now on? If you're ready to make your stay-at-home mom life more "Wonderland" and less "House of Crazy," turn to the next chapter and jump in.

THREE

AT-HOME SELF-CARE BASICS:

AN ACTION PLAN FOR GETTING GOOD NUTRITION, SLEEP, AND PERSPECTIVE

HERE YOU ARE in the At-Home Self-Care Basics chapter, so that means you've identified yourself as a potential candidate for better self-care. Most of us are candidates for better self-care. Welcome! It's time to make a change. The first step in successful behavior change is the creation of a plan. Jump blindly into making big changes in your life and there is a good chance you will balk when you encounter unexpected barriers, or become overwhelmed and lose steam when you don't know the next step to take.

Of course, you can face those same challenges simply in attempting to make a plan, which is why I've done that part for you. This chapter gives you a detailed, easy-to-follow, step-by-step, manageable, yet results-oriented Action Plan for good self-care.

For the purposes of this Action Plan, let's think for a moment about the main areas of basic self-care necessary for good health and well-being. As a psychologist specializing in women's health and wellness, I often focus with my clients on the following six areas:

✓ Good nutrition (including healthy eating, vitamins, hydration)

✓ More/better sleep

✓ Time for yourself (alone time, social time, or hobby)

✓ Self-presentation (primping and preening, mama style—whatever that means to you)

✓ Exercise and fitness

✓ Effective stress/mood management

You may come up with others in addition to these, but these issues are among the most important when it comes to taking care of ourselves as moms. Of these six areas, the last two are addressed in chapters of their own, so let's focus on areas one through four here, devoting four weeks to each goal for a comprehensive, four-month Action Plan that includes making a small change each day or week.

If one of these goals is a more pressing problem area for you than the others, feel free to skip a section and complete only those months of the Action Plan that are relevant to you. I'm starting with nutrition in Month One, but if your diet is fantastic and you're not trying to wean yourself from a serious Goldfish cracker and Diet Coke habit, find the section of the Action Plan that applies to you and start there.

Month One: Good Nutrition

Let's face it: eating well is a challenge for many of us, stay-at-home moms or not. But the unique challenges of becoming a mother, and then entering stay-at-home motherhood, can make healthy eating even tougher to master.

First you're battling the baby weight, coping with the extra pounds that stick around post-pregnancy. You're sleeping (a lot) less, and sleep deprivation has been shown to be associated with greater appetite and (groan) subsequent weight gain. Later on you're balancing toddler or preschooler or school-ager tastes (mac-and-cheese, anyone?) with your own dietary needs, and you're short on time to cook from scratch. Packaged, convenience foods become a whole lot more appealing when you're throwing a snack into your bag on the way to playgroup or navigating the witching hour of dinner-prep crankiness. Plus, your workplace is now your own home, which includes 24-hour access to the pantry, refrigerator, and freezer. It can be tough to resist mindless grazing and multiple afternoon snacks when the cookies and crackers are just steps away.

But hold up, mamas. We've already discussed why it's important to take care of your health, and good nutrition is arguably the most integral component of that. It's worth it to tweak your daily life to make good nutrition possible. The rewards will be greater energy, better health, fewer illnesses, and teaching your children good eating habits by modeling them yourself.

I include healthy foods, multivitamins/supplements, and proper hydration in the category of "good nutrition." Following the "start small" dictum, we'll break the goal down into daily, weekly, and monthly behavior changes. Also, following the "one thing at a time" dictum, I advise that if you're working on good nutrition, you hold off on tackling exercise, sleep, and anything else for the time being, unless things really take off for you and these things come naturally. If not, there is plenty of time to get to all those other aspects of self-care. Focus on your daily diet first, and that success will give you the momentum to improve your self-care in other areas of your life.

One last caveat, please: I am neither a medical professional nor a registered dietitian. I'm a health professional and a long-time avid runner with a lot of knowledge about nutrition and health, but only your own physician can give you individualized advice.

Week 1 Goal: Take Your Vitamins.

Sure, in an ideal world we'd get all our vitamins, minerals, and antioxidants through diet alone. But you're a busy at-home mom; you need some insurance in the form of a good women-specific multivitamin, and perhaps, an additional calcium/vitamin D supplement and/or any other supplements necessary for your own situation. (Here's where you should consult your physician or a registered dietitian about your specific situation if you're unsure of what you need, please.)

Day 1:

We're starting easy, here. (Remember those "success experiences"?) On Day 1, all I ask is that you procure some vitamins for yourself, if you don't already have some in the house. Go to the drugstore, plunk some money down, and feel good that you're investing in your health.

Days 2-7:

On Days 2 through 7, take your vitamin every day. Put the bottle somewhere that you'll see it every day so you won't forget. Or, take it at the same time you give your children their Flintstones chewables. Make it a habit, and keep it up as you tackle Week 2 and beyond.

Week 2 Goal: Drink More Water.

[Reminder: keep taking your vitamins this week, and beyond.]

When my first daughter was born, I shunned caffeine religiously while breastfeeding, but by the time baby number two came along, Diet Coke and coffee were my personal saviors—at the expense of my water consumption. It wasn't pretty. I've since consciously upped my water intake and definitely see and feel the difference in terms of my energy level, complexion, and physical stamina. You will too.

The U. S. Department of Agriculture's Dietary Guidelines for Americans, 2010 (found on the web at ChooseMyPlate.gov), advises that, for better health and nutrition, Americans replace all sugary beverages with water. The idea is that, if it's not low- or nonfat milk or water (or another clear, unsweetened beverage, like herbal tea), it's something you're drinking for pleasure rather than nutrition. And while the occasional "treat" beverage (think soda, juice, and those sugary coffee drinks that are so hard to resist) is fine, it should be just that: occasional. Once you've replaced any purely-for-pleasure beverages with water, you may find that you're still not drinking enough water to stay properly hydrated and healthy, and may need to add in other glasses of water throughout your day.

Days 1-7:

Unless you're already drinking a fair to good amount of water, on each of these days I want you to drink one more glass of water than you are currently drinking. If you're currently drinking juice, soda, or any other "treat" beverages, this would mean that each day you replace one more of those drinks with a glass of water instead. In other words, on Sunday, add one extra glass of water to your daily routine (replacing one sugary drink, if applicable). On Monday, add another one (again, swapping out one more sugary drink) for a total of two more glasses of water than you were previously drinking. On Tuesday, you're up to three additional glasses of water (maybe also three sugary drinks eliminated). And so on.

Now, if you started out already drinking, say, six glasses of water a day, you're not going to want to increase your water consumption to 13 glasses by the end of the week. So adjust these goals accordingly to your own situation. Perhaps, for example, you'll want to increase your water consumption by one extra glass every two days instead. Add lemon wedges or cucumber slices to your water if you need a fresh flavor boost, carry a water bottle with you wherever you go—whatever it takes to help you down as much water as you need.

By the end of Week 2, you should be drinking at least seven glasses of water per day, and ideally more like eight to ten–and doing so in place of downing those types of drinks that aren't so good for you and add extra calories to boot. As before, maintain this new behavior as you move on into Week 3 of your campaign to improve your nutrition.

Week 3 Goal: Whole Grains In, Refined Carbs Out.

[Reminder: keep taking your vitamins and drinking more water this week, and beyond.]

This goal may seem hard, but I swear it's not as daunting as it may sound. I'm not asking for 100% whole-grain perfection here; after all, a life without the occasional bag of Cheetos is seriously not worth living. But there's no getting around the fact that if you want to shed baby weight (even if your baby is six years old), keep your insides in good shape, and protect against diseases like diabetes and cancer, you've got to eat more brown rice, oatmeal, and whole-wheat bread than white bagels and Chips Ahoy.

You say you don't like the taste of whole grains? I say you haven't tried enough of them, and also that our tastes change over time. The brown rice you find too grainy today will seem deliciously nutty and chewy once you wean yourself off processed white grains. Also, lots of women find it easier to gradually make the switch rather than doing a full swap right off the bat: mixing brown rice with white, for example, and gradually reducing the white, or cutting less-healthy processed breakfast cereal with a scoop of whole-grain Grape Nuts or raisin bran in the bowl.

You're not sure what's whole-grain and what's not? Many grocery store items now feature bold labels touting their whole-grain status, so look for that. And with packaged foods, you can check the label and look for "whole-grain" or "whole-wheat" as the first ingredient. In general, we're talking brown instead of white (bread, rice, flour), "heartier" cereals (bran flakes instead of Rice Krispies), and wholesome foods such as oatmeal and popcorn.

Day 1:

If you don't have whole-grain foods in the house, get to the supermarket sometime today to stock up on a few easy ones: whole-grain bread for sandwiches and toast, a canister of oatmeal, a package or two of whole-grain crackers or brown rice cakes, a bag of brown rice or ground flaxseed. (Flaxseed can be added to cereal, muffin batter, pancake batter, smoothies, and homemade cookie dough, and is hardly noticeable beyond a pleasantly nutty, slightly more wholesome taste, yet adds healthy omega-3s, fiber, and protein to your food.)

You can also try some of the packaged foods that are now made from whole grain, such as certain breakfast cereals, tortillas, and pita bread. You're going to be working on incorporating more whole grains into your diet this week, and then continuing to do so in the future, so you need these foods available in your pantry. Remember the ground rule about creating an environment that encourages your desired behavior, i.e., engaging in "stimulus control"? This is it.

Day 2:

Eat breakfast (even if you have not up to now), and in this meal, incorporate some amount of whole-grain food. This could be a slice of whole-wheat toast instead of white or refined wheat toast, a bowl of oatmeal instead of corn flakes, or a sprinkling of ground flaxseed on your yogurt or in a fruit smoothie. It could be granola made with oats. It could be a whole-grain bagel with cream cheese. You choose, but add some whole grains into your very first meal of the day.

Day 3:

Continue with your breakfast goal, and substitute one refined/processed snack today with a healthier whole-grain choice. Whole-grain crackers instead of Cheez-Its? Popcorn instead of potato chips? Low-fat granola instead of candy? You decide.

Day 4:

Repeat Days 2 and 3 to get your bearings before you move on. Spend ten minutes considering a dinner recipe or two that incorporates whole grains rather than refined carbohydrates.

Day 5:

Continue with your Days 2 and 3 goals, and also move on to lunch. Add a whole-grain item to your lunch today, instead of its refined cousin. This could be as simple as whole-grain bread for your turkey sandwich.

Days 6-7:

Continue with your previous daily goals, and cook with whole grains for dinner these days. Remember, this does not have to be complicated or distasteful: whole-grain soft tortillas wrapped around burrito or taco fillings are just as delicious as white flour tortillas, whole-wheat penne or rotini pasta added to vegetable or chicken soup instead of white noodles will be nearly unnoticeable, and whole grain cornbread instead of a white baguette next to a bowl of chili will be gobbled up, I promise.

By the end of this week, you will have added more whole grains to your diet and therefore reduced your consumption of refined carbohydrates—go, you!—but remember: You don't have to eat all whole grains, all the time. The goal is to increase your whole grain consumption while decreasing the amount of less healthy refined carbs you eat, but that doesn't mean you and your family have to swear off French bread, plain bagels, or Ritz crackers completely or forever—let alone birthday cake or the occasional chocolate chip cookie. You don't need whole grains in place of every carbohydrate you're currently eating, just many to most. Continue to follow and work on the above guidelines and you'll be doing fine.

Week 4 Goal: The Ultimate in Good Nutrition—50% Fruits and Veggies.

[Reminder: keep taking your vitamins, drinking more water, and substituting whole grains for many of your processed carbs this week, and beyond.]

You knew it was coming, right? The prescription to nix the cookies and chips in favor of apple slices and bell pepper strips? Well, sure. We all know the key to a healthy diet is plenty of fruits and vegetables—more than most of us are currently getting—in place of some of our burgers, fries, ice cream, and chocolate. (Here is where I confess that when I was nursing my ravenous second daughter, I developed a serious addiction to Hershey's Nuggets. Suggest I snack on baby carrots or cherry tomatoes and I might have smacked you upside the head. I'm happy to say I've moved on to healthier dietary territory.)

We'd all love to snack on Hershey's Nuggets all day long (or is that just me?), but that's just not stellar self-care. Also? You really will feel a million times healthier and more energetic when you're eating more fruits and veggies. You don't have to give up every sweet treat out there. You just need to work toward eating fewer treats and more produce.

The current recommendations from the federal government's MyPlate campaign deal with proportion rather than numbers of servings. The goal is for fruits and vegetables to make up *at least half* of every meal and snack. In other words, if you're sitting down to a meal, half your plate should be filled with fruits and/or vegetables; the other half should be split between protein and grains. If you're having a snack, at least half of what you're eating should be a fruit or a vegetable, or both.

Keep in mind that "at least half" also means that "all" is okay. So for example, a recommended snack may be one apple with one string cheese (i.e., half your snack is fruit), but it may also be just one apple, or only a raw veggie plate. In the latter cases, you're choosing to make your snack 100% produce, which is, by definition, "at least half."

So, while serving size and number remain important—it's still not advised to fill half of an oversized plate with produce and the other half with a burger that's twice the size (and calories) of an appropriate protein and grains choice—our daily goals here are going to focus on slowly working toward that magic 50%. If you don't know how big a "serving" should be, the ChooseMyPlate.gov website is a great place to look—for any food group. Abide by suggested serving sizes; just make sure that whatever their size, your proportions follow the general guideline of at least 50% fruits and vegetables.

Days 1-2:

How many servings of fruits and vegetables are you currently getting each day? One? Three? Five on a good day? None unless you count fruit snacks or the sauce on your pizza? (You actually can count the pizza sauce.) One way to reach that magic 50% at each meal and snack is to go at it one meal or snack at a time. Today, pick one meal or snack to consist of at least half fruits and/or vegetables. It doesn't matter which one; choose one that seems doable to you.

You're still eating a whole grain at breakfast, right? How about adding a cup of berries to your cup of oatmeal? A sliced banana on top of your peanut butter-topped whole-wheat toast? Or maybe adding some baby carrots to your typical afternoon-snack handful of crackers seems simpler to start. If you don't have enough fresh or frozen fruits and vegetables in your house already to start eating more of them, visit the market today too, and get some of your favorites.

Days 3-4:

Pick another meal or snack to add produce to today. If your typical lunch is a turkey sandwich and a piece of fruit, add a helping of vegetables to your plate, and—voila!—half protein and grains (your sandwich), half fruits and veggies. Serving chicken for dinner? Keep your meat and grains to moderately-sized servings, and fill the other half of your plate with a big salad. Or down a glass of 100% vegetable juice in place of that mid-morning Frappuccino. (You can do this to increase your vegetable intake, even with the water rule. Just make sure you keep drinking water also.) Easy—you're up to two meals now.

Day 5:

Apply that 50% rule to one more meal or snack. (Maintain the improvements you've made in the other two, as well.)

Days 6-7:

If you still have any meals or snacks that need more fruits and vegetables, continue to modify those on these two days. By the end of this week, you'll notice that you could start a compost heap or nourish a flock of chickens with all the produce ends you'll be collecting—but, oh, what a great problem to have.

Ideally, you're not just adding these foods into your diet, you're (at least some of the time) eating them instead of junk food, sugary food, or additional starches. Again, I didn't say to give up all those things (I would be murderous without my ice cream). Just try to give most the boot, while you instead indulge in delicious fresh-fruit smoothies, crunchy sugar snap peas, and finger-food edamame. You'll raise children who don't know anything different.

Month One Recap

If you've been following your Action Plan religiously, you have finished Month One in a much better state, nutrition-wise, than when you started. Bravo for you, busy mom! You're taking vitamins/supplements daily, keeping your body and brain well hydrated, eating more whole grains in place of refined carbohydrates, and feeding your body more nutrient- and antioxidant-packed fruits and veggies. You probably feel more energetic than before, you're modeling good nutrition to your children, and you can tackle your stay-at-home mom tasks with vitality. Now keep doing it.

Have you struggled? Don't hesitate to repeat Month One from the beginning, or take an extra month to cement your new nutritional habits before moving on. There's no time limit on taking better care of yourself!

Month Two: Better Sleep

Remember before you had kids, and you didn't yet know that you'd never get a solid, uninterrupted night's sleep again? Ah, those were wonderfully naïve days, weren't they? Did you ever give your nightly eight hours a second thought back then? Your weekend sleep-late mornings? Your—gasp—Sunday afternoon naps? Of course not! Why would you? One of the great cruelties of adulthood is the lack of sleep that flattens you like a bug in the road once you become a parent, and the way you really have no idea about it beforehand. Of course, it's a good thing you don't. If you knew, you might nix the whole idea of having any babies at all.

Of course the sleep deprivation is worst during the postpartum haze of Project Newborn, when you're nursing or bottle-feeding the baby at regular intervals around the clock, sweet dreams be damned. But the harsh truth for many moms is that full nights of sleep never really return once the baby has been night-weaned. Babies, toddlers, and children still wake up and cry, or call for us, in the middle of the night. They have bad dreams; they get too hot; they lose their blankets and need re-tucking in. They vomit. (Why does stomach flu always hit children in the middle of the night?) They get fevers and croup and the kind of stuffed-up colds that make it hard for them to breathe. They decide that five a.m. is a perfectly acceptable time to wake up for the day. And all of this means less sleep for you.

Then there's that eerie way our mama brains tend to jolt us awake at the slightest noise—or even the obsessive *anticipation* of a noise—even when no one's crying or throwing up or calling for a drink of water. I swear, for years after I weaned my last baby, I would wake up at two a.m., and again at four a.m., as if all those months of night-nursing had etched a permanent neurological groove in my brain, a phantom alarm clock singing *Time to feed the baby!* even when there was no such nursing baby, no such dark-of-the-night cry. It drove me crazy.

And what about the sheer fact of not enough time in the day to complete everything you want to get done, and the extra-late bedtime or pre-dawn wake-up as a result? How many of you routinely run after your babes all day on a mere five or six hours of sleep, simply because you're madly trying to fit childcare, housecleaning, cooking, household-running, laundry, exercise, quality time with your partner, friends, and family, pleasure reading, birthday party planning, TV watching, and the occasional indulgence in a hobby into a too-short day? You may not be a go-go career woman anymore, but that doesn't mean you're not burning the candle at both ends in a new way.

It takes its toll. We've all been there. Here's my description of one exhausted period in my stay-at-home mothering life, when my daughters were almost two and four years old:

> *Genevieve woke up crying several times during the night on both Sunday and Monday, so by the end of the day yesterday I was Comatose Mama. Zombie Mama. Don't Talk to Me and I'm Sure We'll All Be Fine Mama.*
>
> *When my husband got home from work, I was outside in the backyard supervising Julia, Genevieve, and their little neighbor friend swimming, running through the sprinkler, slipping down the Little Tikes mini-slide*

into the splash pool, making castles in the sand table, and drawing with sidewalk chalk. We had been out there, all of us, doing all that, for more than an hour in the 90-degree, high-humidity heat, and let me tell you, people: singlehandedly supervising a 22-month-old, a four-year-old, and a five-year-old amidst water, concrete, and a nearby county highway, especially when at least two of the children are very over-tired, ISN'T EXACTLY RELAXING. Oh sure—on the surface it might sound easy enough, but remember: 22 months, four years old, five years old. We're not talking about watching a trio of seven-year-olds entertaining each other. This is still high-maintenance child-minding.

I was doing okay, you understand, and had not yet slipped up and raised my voice or threatened to turn off the sprinkler for the remainder of the summer, but I had definitely slipped into an exhausted state of mind I like to call Survival Mode, which involves conserving all energy by no longer verbally responding to anyone about anything. The second Christopher stepped onto the patio, I believe I said something like, "The rules are: no more water in the sand table; no jumping off or walking down the slide into the pool; no teddy bears or blankies in the sand table in fact they shouldn't even be outside but whatever; and ENOUGH ALREADY WITH DUMPING SAND IN THE POOL!" rather than saying "Hello, how are you, hot day isn't it?" And then I beat it inside.

I was so tired that after dinner I fell asleep sitting up while watching the TV news.

But then I lay awake in bed until after 11 p.m., kept up by the heat and the light and Genevieve crying out in her crib again. And woke up before five, from the sun coming up and the birds singing and Genevieve crying out in her crib (again).

This is why I live on coffee and Diet Coke, people. I'm not saying it's healthy.

Sound familiar?

Mamas, sleep is really, really important. It's linked to appetite, and weight, and heart health, and blood pressure, and memory, and stress level, and safety, and mood. Nothing feels as good or goes as well when your sleep is dysregulated. So let's work on this.

But first, keep in mind that your ideal amount of sleep may be different from mine. While most health experts, such as the Mayo Clinic, recommend seven to nine hours of sleep per night for adults, sleep needs can vary depending on age, sleep quality, previous sleep deprivation, and the like. Let your fatigue level be your guide; if you're exhausted during the day, you need to get more sleep. When you feel generally rested most of the time, you're getting enough sleep for you, whether that's more or less than your friend, sister, or neighbor needs.

Week 1 Goal: Set Yourself Up For Sleep.

In the field of health psychology, a person's sleep habits are called her "sleep hygiene." No, no, I'm not talking about how often you change the sheets or if you remember to floss every night before you go to sleep. Sleep hygiene is all those things you do (or don't do) that affect your sleep quality. Many of these things are within your control, and thus can be altered as needed.

This week is all about stimulus control: adjusting all the controllable things in your environment to make quality sleep more likely (i.e., improving your sleep hygiene). Do what applies to you, and skip anything that doesn't fit your situation.

Day 1:

Spend a few minutes casing your bedroom for any and all sources of light, down to the tiniest glow. Light, even small amounts, inhibits the production of melatonin, the hormone responsible for sleepiness. To sleep well, you want your bedroom as dark as an upscale hotel room. Have an alarm clock with an LED display? Turn it backward or lay it face down on your bedside table. Still in the baby-monitor phase? Flip it light-side toward the wall. TV remotes with glow-in-the-dark buttons, slits of light sneaking in from the curtains, the errant glow of a bathroom nightlight. All of these can disrupt sleep more than you'd imagine.

Day 2:

Consider white noise. If you're a light sleeper like I am, and wake up from even the faintest normal household or outside sounds, white noise may be your miracle worker. It seems counter-intuitive, but adding constant, low, soothing noise can promote sleep by masking the unpredictable night noises that jar you awake. You can buy white noise machines at stores or online—I swear by mine, the SleepMate™—but you can also use a box fan or even keep a nearby bathroom fan switched on. If easy waking is an issue for you, try some form of white noise tonight. It may take some getting used to, so give it a few nights before you decide if it's right for you or not.

Day 3:

Cut out the afternoon and evening caffeine. This can be a hard one, but caffeine hangs around the body for hours after you've ingested it, so try your hardest not to indulge from mid-afternoon on. And yes (sigh), that means chocolate too. This change needs to continue from here on out.

Day 4:

Cool down the room. Is your bedroom cool enough for optimal sleep? We all sleep better at a cooler temperature. Turn down the thermostat a bit, making sure the kids are sufficiently bundled, turn on the ceiling fan, or take that extra blanket off the bed.

Days 5-7:

Start thinking about what activities prevent you from getting to bed earlier than you currently do. Do you stay up late watching TV? Reading? Surfing the Internet? Do you spend your evening completing household tasks, and thus preclude a healthy bedtime schedule because your downtime doesn't begin until 10 p.m.? Think about what you can jettison, decrease, or reschedule so that next week you can get serious about getting to bed early.

Week 2 Goal: Go to Bed (A Little Bit) Earlier.

You may not be able to control if or how often your children wake up (and wake you up) overnight, but you can control your bedtime to maximize the chances of more hours of sleep per night.

Days 1-7:

This week, go to bed 15 minutes earlier than usual. Maintain this small increment of extra sleep every night in order to solidify the habit. The idea is to make a small change at first, one that will be painless and easily attainable. Baby steps, remember?

Week 3 Goal: Go to Bed (Even) Earlier.

You've probably guessed where I'm going this week. Harness your positive momentum, and keep going. Remember, you're moving toward an end result of rested, energetic mornings—which will make your daily challenges easier to handle. It's worth the effort, and well within your reach.

Days 1-7:

This week, move your bedtime up by 15 more minutes, so that now you're turning out the light 30 minutes earlier than you typically did before you started the Action Plan. You should notice a real difference in how you feel this week, with an added half hour of sleep every night and continued attention to darkness, white noise, and bedroom temperature. Assess how you feel with this slight nightly sleep increase; do you still wake up exhausted each day, or struggle to maintain alertness and energy during daylight hours? Do you feel rested in the morning?

Week 4 Goal: Continue Your Progress.

If your former bedtime was truly super-late, keep moving up your bedtime this week, and for as long as you like until you're getting enough sleep at night. You'll know when you've hit it because you'll wake easily in the morning and feel rested during the day.

Days 1-7:

This week, repeat your previous success. Go to bed another 15 minutes earlier, for a total of 45 minutes earlier than your old bedtime. Continue to maintain your new, earlier bedtime, and feel more rested for life.

Month Two Recap

By the end of this month, if you've followed the Action Plan as described, you've taken huge steps toward feeling energetic, rested, and ready for each day with your kids by improving your sleep hygiene and changing your bedtime schedule. Talk about an improvement in self-care! Giving yourself the best sleep possible for your situation (new mamas: hang in there!) is an incredibly important way of taking better care of yourself.

And while I can't promise that your toddler won't wake up at five a.m., or that your baby will sleep through the night, I can tell you with confidence that if you're exhausted much of the time, a darker, cooler room, white noise, and an earlier bedtime will help you get better sleep, giving you a boost of physical and mental energy, and restoring some emotional resilience. Don't worry; you can sleep in on weekends and nap on Sunday afternoons when your children go off to college.

Month Three: Time for Yourself

Stay-at-home moms are in the unique work situation of never being truly "off duty" or even being able to walk away from the workplace on a regular basis. Can you think of any other job that includes 24/7 shifts, no vacation days, no distinction between weekdays and weekends, and a work environment that follows you wherever you go?

Of course there are amazing positive aspects of this job, including freedom and flexibility at important times, the lack of a dress code, and the relief and satisfaction that comes from being the primary adult in your children's days. Those are some great benefits! But time for yourself is not one of them. Any job that requires you to routinely allow other people to accompany you on your bathroom visits is pretty brutal when it comes to respect for your personal needs.

It's rough, but most of us get used to it. Many of us get so used to it, in fact, that after a while we fail to seek out ways to get those personal needs met, as if we've forgotten what it's like to take a bubble bath without an audience or do something other than chores and errands on a Saturday morning. I still remember what I wrote on my blog the first time I experienced a few hours per week to myself, the autumn that one daughter went off to kindergarten every morning and the other started nursery school for five hours a week:

> The conversation at playdate last week went something like this:
>
> Me: So Genevieve starts preschool next week, Tuesday and Thursday mornings.

Full-Time Working-Mom Friend: Wow! That's right! You'll get five hours per week without kids at home! Oh, my gosh, that must seem like a dream after five years of small children attached to your hip every waking moment!

Me: Well, actually, Julia's school gets out a half-hour earlier than Genevieve's so it won't actually be five hours without kids...

Friend: Oh. Okay, so...four hours per week.

Me: It's actually down to more like three.

Friend: What?! Dear God, why?

Me: Eh. A complicated set of factors related to the school bus drop-off schedule and Genevieve's preschool pick-up time. I've got to pick Julia up at the school on Tuesdays and Thursdays. I mean, I know that's still a one-hour-and-forty-minutes-or-so block of time alone two times per week that I've never had before so I shouldn't be complaining, but...

Friend: Are you kidding me? It is physically painful to hear that kind of subtraction math! That time is like gold!

Me: I have a feeling an hour and a half–or whatever–will fritter away in the blink of an eye and all my plans for what to do with that time will disappear. I mean, you come in from preschool drop-off, you switch the laundry over, grab your second cup of coffee, answer a phone call, check your e-mail, clean up from breakfast, and poof! It's time to head out to the elementary school. I love being with my daughters, but I have personal goals I was hoping to start working on during that time.

Friend: I think your personal goal should be to walk in from preschool drop-off, proceed directly to the nearest chair, and sit there. The entire time. Resting. In silence.

Me: I don't think I know how to do that.

Friend: GOLD, Shannon. GOLD.

See? You forget what to do with yourself beyond the nonstop daily agenda of childcare and household management. You get so accustomed to having no time for yourself that it starts to feel normal. But that kind of "normal" eventually leads to burnout and resentment, mamas, as we've already discussed.

It's okay. All it means is that we've got to consciously make time for ourselves—you've got to consciously make time for yourself—to enjoy kid-free social time with friends, couple time with your sweetheart, your favorite hobby, or just some solo relaxation.

Get ready—this is going to be a fun month.

Week 1 Goal: Reclaim the Grown-Up Playdate.

Don't you miss conversing with friends without being interrupted ten times a minute by knee-high individuals who drool? Or maybe even having time to get together with friends at all? Calling hello out the car window to the other moms in the carpool line does not count as social time, in case you were wondering.

You don't need me to lay out any daily goals for this task. All you need to do this week is find time for at least one hour of kid-free socializing with a good girlfriend (or a group of good girlfriends!). I don't care how you do it, who watches your children while you do it, or what you decide to do during your time. Meet a friend for lunch while your kids are in school, sneak out after their bedtime for a glass of wine while your partner minds the family; turn your Saturday run into a group affair. Whatever sounds fun and doable. Think of it as a grown-up playdate, and consider it a sanity-saving requirement. You deserve an uninterrupted conversation.

Now: can you imagine doing this every week? Try it.

Week 2 Goal: Go on a Date.

Remember that person with whom you started this whole parenthood gig? Seen him much lately other than when you hand the baby off to him at the end of the day? Done anything with him recently that wasn't in the company of your children? (And I don't mean folding the laundry at 10 p.m. with the baby monitor on in the background.)

That's what I thought.

Don't worry, moms, I understand. I've been there too! (I'm actually still there a little too often.) It's completely comprehensible why alone time with your spouse would get deleted from the to-do list when there's so much to do to keep your house running smoothly and your children healthy, safe, and happy. There are only so many hours in a day!

I get it. But this week you're going to find—make—the time to have a little date with your honey. Pick a night (or day), tell your spouse, and plan something. The conventional version of this is to book a sitter and go off to dinner or a movie (or both!). And if you can do that, wonderful. But if budgetary or childcare-related problems plague you, the easy version is to put the babies to bed, pop in a movie, and break out the wine (or popcorn, or Junior Mints). A DVD and the couch can make a routine evening into a date, provided you make it a priority to think of it that way.

So: again, no daily goals this week. Just a nudge to plan and go on—or stay in for—one date this week. Remind yourself who you made those babies with, and why. Tend to your marriage, and you'll be tending to your emotional well-being.

Once again, consider this a weekly habit. Add one low-stress date to your weekly hour of friend time. You are worthy of both friendship and a happy marriage.

Week 3 Goal: Rediscover a Hobby.

If someone had asked me what my favorite hobby was during my first year of at-home motherhood, I probably would have said eating chocolate while watching *Oprah* and nursing the baby, counting down the minutes until my husband came home from work and trying not to cry. Grim.

My first postpartum period was full of colic, breastfeeding complications, ER visits, and milk pore infections (if you don't already know about this, you really don't want to). It's safe to say that for a long, long time—maybe even my daughter's entire first year of life—my resources were stretched so thin that there was no part of me able to consider interests or activities outside the realm of mothering. However, the summer Julia turned one I tentatively dipped my toes back into running, my long-time favorite hobby that I had not revisited since my pre-pregnancy days. I had a jogging stroller, given to us when Julia was born, so one sunny July afternoon I changed into workout clothes, strapped the baby into the reclining seat, and hit the sidewalks of my south Minneapolis neighborhood, huffing and puffing and nervously peering through the plastic window on the top of the stroller sunshade to see if Julia was doing okay. It felt great.

There have been times since then when I've been again unable to engage in this hobby. When Genevieve was born and my days were spent nursing an infant while chasing after a toddler, thus burning more calories than I could reliably take in, I would have said my favorite hobby was eating. I'm happy to say that running is still and again my most beloved hobby, one I take time for several times a week. And now I go all by myself.

Do you have a favorite hobby you've let languish during your busy stay-at-home mom days? I'll bet you do, and even if you can't think of one right now, I know you can come up with one. Think about what you'd do (besides nap) if you were suddenly given an extra free hour per week. Read a great novel? Cook? Scrapbook? Garden, go for a walk, draw, paint, write?

This week your task is to spend an hour on a hobby. If you're short on solo evening/weekend time, use your children's naptime (cleaning the bathrooms can wait!) or school hours. It doesn't matter what your hobby is, only that it's fun for you and does not involve taking care of anyone else. And if you can devote more than an hour to it, all the better.

An hour a week of attention to an interest outside of parenting will do wonders for your mental health. We all need activities in our lives that stimulate our minds, bring us joy, and give our bodies and brains a break from all things motherhood-related. Give yourself permission to do something fun each week.

Week 4 Goal: Give Yourself Some R & R.

Taking time for yourself to merely relax—to take a bubble bath or a nap or get a massage or your nails done—can be the hardest thing of all for a busy stay-at-home mom. But if there's any part of self-care you need and deserve to engage in on a very regular basis, it's the gift of some rest and relaxation, because it's probably the thing you experience the least in a typical stay-at-home mom day, and yet it's integral to mental health. If you're still night-nursing a tiny babe, no doubt the mere words "rest and relaxation" can feel like a slap in the face, but, honestly, before long it will get easier, though even moms of grade-schoolers often struggle to make time for the soul-feeding pleasure of a mama time-out.

It doesn't need to be long, it doesn't have to cost money, and it doesn't even have to take place outside the confines of your house. (Although it can be all these things.) Ten minutes for some calm deep breathing. Half an hour during naptime for a magazine (or a nap!). An early-a.m. cup of coffee on the porch before the troops wake up. A daily check-in phone call with your best fellow-stay-at-home-mom girlfriend. And, occasionally, that massage, or that mani-pedi appointment, or a weekend afternoon to yourself to do whatever strikes your fancy.

Days 1-7:

Every day this week, give yourself some rest and relaxation time. It can be ten minutes; it can be an hour—although probably a shorter stint is easier to incorporate into your stay-at-home mama life on a daily basis. And make this separate from your regular social time, date night, and time for a hobby. These things may qualify as rest and relaxation, but this week we're focusing on the more intimate, whatever-gets-you-through gestures that help you conquer the busyness of your daily life and recharge your batteries for the next adventure. I *know* you can give yourself ten minutes a day for pure relaxation. And I guarantee that, if you do, you'll find yourself facing the day with renewed energy and better perspective.

Month Three Recap

Wow, mama! How do you feel? You've spent an entire month working on time for yourself in every possible form. You've experimented with making dates with friends, making dates with your honey, enjoying a hobby, and letting yourself rest.

Hopefully, you've worked on including these things on a weekly basis (and that last one, on a daily basis). But you will need, as time goes on, to find a schedule that works for you and your family. Maybe date night needs to be once or twice a month instead of every week; if you're going from never to once a month, that's still a success. Maybe an hour with a girlfriend can be combined with a hobby, and you and your buddy can enjoy each other's company while you also run, walk, scrapbook, knit, or whatever fun activity suits you both.

It's all good. It's all mama self-care. It will fill up your cup and allow you to continue your path of stay-at-home mom-hood with more energy and enthusiasm than before.

Month Four: Self-Presentation (Primping and Preening, Mama Style)

Do the words "mama" and "style" seem contradictory to you? Is your idea of "style" a day when you manage to pull on yoga pants rather than stay in pajama pants?

As a woman who once, a month or two postpartum with the aforementioned challenging baby number one, went for an entire stroller walk around the neighborhood, stopping to chat with a middle-aged father of grown kids, not noticing that I had forgotten to re-fasten my nursing bra on the right and so was no doubt flopping and flailing along one-sidedly, one inflated nursing boob properly contained, and the other, well, doing who-knows-what under my thin cotton top—as *that* woman—I understand. I do.

I'm also the woman who, five years into parenthood, during my daughter's first week of kindergarten, had the following conversation with my best friend (who did not yet have a child in elementary school):

Me: Oh my goodness, I am NOT liking this business of having to be up, dressed, and appropriately groomed by 7:50 a.m. for the kindergarten bus stop.

Friend: What? YOU don't have to be ready for the day; only Julia does. You can go back inside and get ready after the bus leaves.

Me: No. I'm out there with my neighbor, who is always totally dressed and looking nice, obviously ready to start her day. I can't be out there at the bus stop in my pajama pants and bathrobe with uncombed hair and no makeup! You want me to be THAT mom?

Friend: I should be your neighbor! I'D be that mom, and then you wouldn't care about being outside in your bathrobe on the sidewalk with your neighbor!

Me: Ha! But you're not.

Friend: I guarantee, in one month you'll be over it. You'll be out there in whatever, coffee cup in hand.

Me: You're probably right.

I'm happy to say that, because I've worked fairly hard over the past few years at scrapping the no-makeup, messy-ponytail, yoga-pants stage that I languished in so long after the births of my babies, I did not, after all, devolve into a pajama-clad mom at the bus stop. *Thank God.* But it was tempting. Because that bus comes *early*. And who wants to think about style at that hour?

Well. But. There's this thing about primping and preening a little bit, and about wearing flattering, stylish clothes, even as a stay-at-home mom. It not only sends a message to the world that you're a pulled-together mom, worthy of respect and ready to conquer the world in your own awesome way, it makes you feel good about yourself. Really!

This month I want you to think about primping and preening as a form of self-care. I want you to think about your style, and how it fits into your life as a stay-at-home mom.

Of course, as the anecdotes above illustrate, mama style is an evolution, and it's highly personal. It's different at different stages. For the newly postpartum, night-nursing mom, anything beyond soft, stretchy nursing tops and comfy, forgiving yoga pants is style overachievement, as far as I'm concerned. When the babies reach toddlerhood, style might mean applying a dash of make-up and embellishing your at-home uniform of jeans and a tee with a chunky bracelet or a bright scarf. And once you hit the school pick-up line (or the kindergarten bus stop), maybe you're moving on into regular salon trims and the occasional manicure, because the kids are in school and you actually have— just maybe—a free hour in the day.

Let's assume that if you're reading this part of the Action Plan, you're not already applying flawless makeup every morning and hitting playgroup in boots and skinny jeans rather than whatever outfit was lying at the foot of your bed when you got dressed in the thirty seconds between making rice cereal and wiping someone's bum. Let's assume that whatever you're doing in the way of (not) primping and (not) preening is unsatisfying to you, and that you'd really like to experiment with allowing a little style back into your daily life, even if that life involves more pretend tea parties than real cocktail parties.

We can do that.

Week 1 Goal: Put on Some Makeup.

How much makeup do you normally wear? Concealer only, to hide those up-all-night circles? Lip gloss and mascara? Nothing unless you're leaving the house that day? Nothing even if you are?

We're all different, and so are our philosophies about makeup. For a year or so after the birth of my first baby, I reveled in no longer working in my therapy office every day—and that meant also reveling in no longer having to wear makeup every day. I also held the now-mysterious (to me, anyway) belief that wearing makeup as a stay-at-home mom—particularly one whose main outings were stroller walks around the block and the occasional visit to the playground at the end of our street—was silly, vain, and somehow not really "hip-mama" enough. Shouldn't I be a freewheeling, super-casual, all-natural mama, digging in the garden with my baby in her bouncy seat under the shade of our giant elm tree? Who needs makeup for that?

But after awhile I realized that, as a super-pale Scandinavian blonde—and an extremely sleep-deprived one at that—going completely barefaced wasn't doing me any favors. And I don't just mean in terms of what other people thought of my outward appearance. I mean when I glimpsed my own wan face in the mirror.

I started applying a little makeup during my stay-at-home mom days. At first, it was only when I was taking the baby to the pediatrician or was headed to my therapy office later in the day when my husband came home from work, but later, even when my day's agenda held nothing more than sitting in my boho-mama-friend Rachel's garden with the babies wading in the splash pool. I noticed it made me feel happier, better about myself, pulled together. It made me feel a little more ready for whatever my day might throw my way.

Later, as my first baby grew, and then my second baby came along and I was busy meeting other at-home moms in our family's new town, I hit my stride and was more able to primp and preen in the mornings. Then I splurged on some boutique makeup and took the time to apply cosmetics most every day. It wasn't because I cared so much what the UPS guy thought of me when I answered the door, but because I cared how I felt as I went about my day. And the truth is, I need a little help in the natural-beauty department, so wearing makeup every day makes me feel better than flaunting the barefaced look. Nothing wrong with that.

This week, I encourage you to do a little more with makeup than you are currently doing. If you're barely able to drag yourself out of bed in the morning and makeup is the last thing on your mind, start with a dash of rosy lip gloss and perhaps a little eye-brightening concealer patted around the inner corners of your eyes. If you're already doing that, try a coat or two of mascara and a swipe of blush. If, like me, you're newly forty and feeling a little less glow-y than you used to be, go get yourself one of those awesome tinted moisturizers and use that under anything else you might apply (as a sparer version of foundation, I mean).

Put on a little makeup every single day this week, even if that means you don't get to it until lunchtime some days. Even if the only person who sees you is the baby and the UPS guy. And especially if you're headed out to playgroup, the bus stop, or the pick-up line. Just try it, and see how it makes you feel. Maybe a little more lovely and polished? I thought so.

Week 2 Goal: Do Your Nails.

I know that the most important things about your hands and feet are the children they carry, the playground slides they guard and swings they push, the carpools they drive. Most days you're probably not thinking about what your nails look like or how long ago you had your last pedicure. I get that, and it's okay. But one of the simple joys of life is, in the middle of a hectic day involving next to no personal time, catching a quick glimpse of your lovely, simply manicured hands or your summery tangerine-hued toes peeking out of your sandals. It's like a wee reminder that you matter, that you're still a woman who takes care of herself, underneath that finger paint, or spit-up-stained nursing top, or BabyBjörn.

It doesn't have to be professionally done or expensive. I get my nails done at a salon just once or twice a year, but from April to October my toenails are continuously painted a rotating palette of drugstore-bought colors. I do it myself, on the living room floor, in the evening, in front of So You Think You Can Dance. As for fingernails, we all know how long polish lasts on hands that spend much of their time diapering, scrubbing, bathing, cooking, and cleaning. (Not long.) However, a little cuticle oil and clear polish go a long way toward making your hands and nails look glossy, pretty, and groomed, while hiding chips and nicks.

This week, I want you to do your nails, or get them done at the salon. Fingers and toes if possible, but if you must choose just one, go for the pedicure since it will last a long time, and the bright color will be cheery to look at. If you're no good at nail-polishing but can't justify the salon expense, maybe a friend can do it for you. Trade her some homemade cookies, or a good cocktail, or whatever your specialty happens to be. It can be mommy social hour, while the kids play! Trust me, it'll be fun. And if you are good at doing your own nails, it can be mommy alone time. Go pick a fun color and get going.

Week 3 Goal: Pretty Up Your Hair.

Now that we've made some progress in the simpler primp-and-preen areas, it's time to take care of that hair.

What do you think about your hair when you look in the mirror? That it looks pretty great considering the fact that you get approximately fifteen seconds every morning to style it? That it looks pretty great, period? (Yay, you!) That you're months overdue for a trim, or a color touch-up, or a new style altogether? That your predictable ponytail is getting old? That it needs help but you can't justify the time, or the expense, or the you-focused mental energy?

I hear you. I've thought all those things about my hair at various times since becoming a mom.

But this week, if you're feeling anything but thrilled about your hair these days, you're going to take action. And that action will be different for each of you. It may mean picking up the phone and scheduling a trim and color. It may mean cutting it all off or getting bangs or breaking out the flat iron. It may mean simply wearing your hair down, instead of in its customary ponytail, two days this week. Or, if you must wear it up, putting it back in a pretty new clip instead of that worn-out elastic band.

Think for a minute about what your beauty goal for your hair would be, were you to focus on it. Because this week you *are* going to focus on it.

Does this seem vain, or inconsequential, or a waste of time? I beg to differ. I think our hair says an awful lot about us. It tells others if we're sporty or girly, if we feel young or old, if we're more traditional or have an edgy slant. Most important of all, it tells others how we feel about giving ourselves time to get ready in the morning—which of course is related to how we feel about giving ourselves time, period. And this, in turn, signals to others about how we expect to be treated.

Take a hair-related action this week, something that will make you feel more beautiful, more polished, more put-together—whatever. See how it makes you feel. Then keep it up. You're worth it.

Week 4 Goal: Inject Some Style into Your Wardrobe.

Oh my, it's time to tackle the Herculean task of breaking out of the yoga-pants-and-t-shirt uniform currently all the rage with stay-at-home moms.

Listen. I know it's tempting, when you're home with babies or kids all day and you spend a lot of time on the floor / at the park / scrubbing toilets, to default to the comfiest option possible, which is generally yoga pants or jeans and a basic tee. But comfiest doesn't have to mean sloppiest. Who says stylish can't be comfy? Who says jeans and a tee can't be a little more than just jeans and a tee? We can work on this.

Mama style doesn't have to be an oxymoron. It doesn't have to mean worn-out jeans and running shoes at all times, or yoga pants at parent-teacher conferences, or never dressing up. But it also doesn't have to be complicated, expensive, or impractical. (As my daughters would say, in an attempt at "I'm serious": "I'm *honest!*") I'm not asking you to revert to the 1950s housewife stereotype, cooking and cleaning in an impeccable shirtdress and heels every single day.

Consider this your week of Dressing Better. And, like the makeup situation, "better" will mean something different to each of you. Better might mean *actual* pants instead of yoga pants. Better might mean a necklace with your jeans and a tee. Better might mean khakis instead of jeans, or a skirt instead of khakis. Better might mean pretty ballet flats instead of those old running shoes you use to work in the garden. A ruffled blouse instead of a plain t-shirt. A belted trench instead of your husband's old fleece. Heck, better might truly mean anything clean, unrumpled, and not something you slept in last night. I *know* you can do better than that.

Take a look at your wardrobe this week, shop your own closet, and see what slightly (or hugely!) nicer pieces you have in there, but that you haven't been wearing because you figure, *Eh, all I'm doing is driving to soccer and going to the supermarket and doing laundry and supervising a backyard playdate, I don't need to look nice.*

You know what? You *do* need to look nice, however you define that word and however you'd characterize your personal style. (Mommy chic? Boho-mama? Grown-up preppy? Sporty? Classic? Trendy?) You need to look nice—at least some of the time!—to remind yourself that moms can look nice. To model self-care to your children (especially your daughters!). To give yourself a boost of energy-producing self-confidence when you spy your reflection in the grocery store doors and realize that even if your toddler has had three tantrums already today and it's not yet ten a.m., you're not falling all to pieces wearing a pile of dirty laundry. To be ready for whatever might come your way that day—because wouldn't you be more willing to accept an impromptu playdate invitation or join the other preschool moms for coffee at the last minute if you were dressed nicely? And wouldn't that be fun?

Sure, you could go out and shop for a whole new, chic, mommy wardrobe, if you had unlimited time, alternate childcare, and a trust fund. But for the rest of us, here are some easy ideas to consider—and try out—for upping your mama-style quotient this week:

- ✓ Try a simple, casual, knee-length day dress instead of jeans and a top one day; it's just as comfortable (really!) as jeans or yoga pants, and it makes getting dressed in the morning even quicker and easier because it's one piece only. Who doesn't love quick and easy?

- ✓ Put a bold necklace over your usual solid tee.

- ✓ Finish off your usual casual outfit with pretty ballet flats or sporty casual slip-ons instead of ratty running shoes, or flip-flops that are better suited to the pool.

- ✓ When the weather turns warm, consider an easy cotton knee-length skirt in place of shorts. It instantly upgrades your look to pretty and pulled-together, yet it's just as cool and easy as uber-casual shorts. And you can definitely wear a casual skirt with the same tees and tanks you're currently pairing with shorts and jeans.

- ✓ Punch up your accessories. A bright new handbag, a colorful patterned scarf, a wide, flowered headband, a retro-preppy tie belt: all are budget-friendly, eye-catching, and add a stylish jolt to your basic mom uniform, yet none require complicated dressing or even dressy situations to justify their wear. (And a large, stylish tote can easily double as a diaper bag.)

That should be enough to get you going. Have fun! I guarantee that dressing a little better than usual this week—maybe getting dressed *period*—will make you feel better about yourself and will probably garner a few compliments too. And when you're dressed prettily in your very *own* version of mom style, you may be more likely to leave your house with the fussy baby, meet up with friends and their kids, grab a coffee, soak up the sunlight, whatever brings you joy.

Month Four Recap

Now that you've stepped up your beauty regimen and paid some much-needed attention to your personal style, you should be looking awesome. More importantly, you should be feeling confident and pleased with yourself, and projecting that confidence and pleasure out into the world. Stay-at-home moms can definitely be stylish on the job. After all, you're the perfect example.

If you've completed any or all of the month-long sections of the Stay-at-Home Mom Self-Care Action Plan, you've taken a huge step in making your daily mothering life healthier and more satisfying. Know that you can return to Chapters 2 and 3 at any time, to reinforce these new habits and give yourself a motivation boost. You've proven that you're capable of taking on some major lifestyle changes in the name of better emotional and physical health, but that doesn't mean you have to get it all right, right at first, or even all the time. Consider this Action Plan your tune-up for body and mind, one you can repeat whenever you need a little coaching to get back into the swing of self-care.

FOUR

AT-HOME FITNESS:

MAINTAINING THE MACHINE

I DON'T KNOW ABOUT YOU, but I have no memories of my mom—a stay-at-home mother (and later a work-at-home mother) in the '70s and '80s—lifting free weights in the living room or racing out the door for a brisk walk or a group fitness class when my dad got home from work. Those weren't the things she did, and I don't remember anyone else's mom doing them either. Boy, have things changed. These days, if we aren't squeezing gym workouts or baby-jogger runs into our busy stay-at-home mom days, we're thinking that we should and feeling guilty when we don't.

We're bombarded every day with news and updates about how to keep our bodies and minds healthy, which kind of exercise is best, how much is optimal and how often is enough. And while this information is valuable and positive, it's also fodder for our ever-lengthening lists of Things To Feel Bad About (if we're not exercising) or Things to Fit In (if we are).

In this chapter I challenge you to look at fitness in a positive light, if you don't already do so. We know more about the benefits of exercise than our mothers did at our age—and that's a good thing. It means we have more knowledge about how to be the agents of our own physical health, as much as is possible. It means we can increase our odds of being around for our children for a very long time.

Those are some of the long-term, big-picture reasons to exercise. But in order to psych yourself up to get started, consider all the immediate and tangible benefits.

What's In It For Me?

You'll lose that baby—or toddler, or preschooler—weight.

Ah, yes. The pregnancy weight. You know, those pounds that stick around long past the postpartum period, sometimes taking up residence for months or even years? Until you can't really call them "baby weight" anymore, unless your definition of "baby" includes all-day kindergarten and size Toddler-12 shoes? Yeah, *those* pounds. Exercise can help you get rid of them once and for all.

And then you won't gain it back.

Once you do drop those pregnancy pounds, you want it to be for good, right? (Or at least until the next pregnancy.) Exercise helps that happen. Believe me, there's nothing better than running enough miles per week to be able to crash on the sofa with the occasional—okay, in my case, the habitual—bowl of ice cream, or enjoy popcorn at the movies (Who am I kidding? Are you going to the movies? Make that: *or order the super-charged mocha with whipped cream as you go through the coffee drive-thru so the baby won't wake up*) without watching the scale creep toward dreaded levels.

Rock that tank top—or those skinny jeans—in the school pick-up line.

There's no denying the toning power of consistent exercise. And since most of us get a little soft around the edges after pregnancy, postpartum recovery, and/or nursing, toning is...um...greatly needed. The good news is that it doesn't take long before regular exercise begins to show its effects. Walking some hills pushing that stroller, cranking out a few push-ups, even if you start on your knees, in front of the TV, biking while pulling the kiddo trailer—they all work your muscles in a big way, and if you do them often enough, your quads, glutes, triceps, and shoulders will show it sooner than you think.

Sure, it's a little vain. Why not let vanity be your motivation to do something great for your health? Whatever works, mamas.

It'll make your life easier.

Here's another thing about those muscles that look so awesome peeking out from under a sundress: they are functional. Yes, being fit makes all those things you do all day as a stay-at-home mom—the lugging of laundry baskets, the toting of babies on your hips, the carrying of groceries and diaper bags and infant car seats—a heck of a lot easier. Wouldn't it be nice to be able to heft the folded-down double stroller into the back of your SUV without feeling like you either need to go lie down or visit the chiropractor?

You know that one mom you always see around your neighborhood or at the park or as you drive around town, the one propelling a jogging stroller one-handedly as she runs up hills, or walking a dog while wearing a baby backpack and toting a shopping bag, looking capable and strong and NOT huffing and puffing? That can be you.

It relieves the stress of sleep-training the baby · listening to the baby cry · weaning the baby · potty-training the baby · sending the baby off to kindergarten · insert your favorite stressor here.

I know it can be hard to get off the sofa and out the door the second you have the opportunity. At those moments, staying seated and ingesting chocolate seems like the best idea. But I promise you, getting some exercise will relieve stress much better than eating chocolate on the couch will. Because, think about it: after you eat the chocolate, then you have one more thing to be stressed about! Exercise is an awesome outlet for stress management. (More on this in Chapter 5, by the way.) It lowers cortisol, a hormone in your body that is responsible for all those unpleasant physical sensations of anxiety you may be overly familiar with if you're at all like me: the racing heart, rapid breathing, sweaty palms, knot in your stomach, and that awful revved-up thrumming feeling you get in your torso when you don't know how many more nights of sleep deprivation you can handle.

At any rate, exercise can make all that better. It also helps you sleep better, produces energy to face life's challenges, and forces you to focus for an hour on something other than diapers and bottles and room-parent volunteering. In the end, you'll come home feeling calmer, less stressed, and more able to—once again!—focus on diapers and bottles and room-parent volunteering.

It may be the only "me-time" you'll get this week—or any week.

When you're a mom, alone time is about as rare as the kids sleeping in on a Saturday. There are awesome, fun ways to squeeze in exercise with your kiddos in tow—more on that later in this chapter—but when you can get out of the house on your own, those solitary miles of running or walking or biking can be amazingly restorative. It's nice to hear only the sound of your own breathing, traffic, and birds chirping, rather than the charming-yet-relentless chorus of children screeching, giggling, whining, talking, yelling, crying, and repeating "Mama, watch this!" over and over and over again. As much as we love them, sometimes we need to just walk—or run—away from them.

Once you start viewing your workouts as precious me-time, they take on a whole new meaning. You start to cherish them, look forward to them, and fiercely protect them. They're your only time to take care of you and only you. And it's laudable, impressive time, too, not like a manicure or cocktails with your friends! (Which is not to say there is anything wrong with manicures or cocktails with your friends, ladies.) Who can criticize your determination to complete several solid workouts every week? They're recommended by the U.S. Surgeon General!

I Can't Exercise, Because...

Given all these fabulous reasons for embracing fitness as a stay-at-home mom, you'd think we'd all be out there on a regular basis, putting in our exercise time and feeling great about it. But excuses crop up. Here are some common barriers to exercise:

"I don't have time."

Definitely the most common anti-workout refrain, this one is easy to understand yet challenging to overcome. (But not impossible!) We've already discussed the way stay-at-home mom duties expand to fill every waking moment, and some of our sleeping ones as well. Sometimes it seems like even the absolutely non-negotiables eat up more time than we have in the day, leaving no room for anything optional. I know it's hard to fit in a run when dinner needs to be cooked and the baby needs to be nursed. I'll help you get over that hump.

"I don't have the energy."

Boy oh boy, do I get this one. As the mom of a child who still did not sleep through the night at *four years old*, I'm extremely familiar with exhaustion. We're close personal friends, in fact. So I'm not going to criticize you if you tell me that at the end of the workday you don't have the energy to walk around your dining room table, let alone your neighborhood. But I will ask you to keep reading, and be willing to consider some solutions to your physical fatigue.

"Ugh! I feel way too fat and out of shape to exercise!"

This is a frequent refrain after the postpartum period, when moms tend to be overly critical of their rounder, slower bodies and overly anxious to return to their pre-pregnancy shape. And yes, it's frustrating to feel too out of shape to do the thing that would help us get back into shape. Let's all take a moment to appreciate the irony here. Now let's kick it to the curb and move on.

"I don't have anyone to watch my children."

Another understandable dilemma. Not all of us have in-town parents or in-laws just waiting to take the kids off our hands for an hour a few times a week, or a spouse with a schedule that allows us to get away in the evenings to exercise. There are ways around this. Read on.

"Soooooo unmotivated."

Maybe you've got the childcare, the energy (theoretically), the time (even more theoretically). Maybe it's your own mind that's the obstacle, the thoughts running through your head that say things like, *Aw, just skip it this time*, and *I just don't feel like it today*, or *One workout won't matter one way or the other*. We all have those thoughts at times, and once you're a regular exerciser, it's fine to answer the call of unmotivation once in a while. I myself have been known to skip a run because it's windy, I feel lazy, and there's something good on TV. But lack of motivation can hold you back from some great outcomes. Sometimes you have to willfully generate your motivation. I will show you how.

"I don't have the money for a gym membership, exercise equipment, and/or fancy workout clothes. After all, we're living on one income."

Wouldn't it be nice to have enough disposable income to afford the gym, an at-home treadmill or elliptical for those days you don't feel like leaving the house, and the cute exercise clothes in which to enjoy those things? No doubt some of you do, which is awesome. But for the rest of us, it can be challenging to figure out what equipment or gear is necessary, what's optional, and what we shouldn't spend our money on. Most forms of exercise do cost something, after all, even if only a pair of walking shoes. But it doesn't have to be prohibitive.

"I'm dealing with postpartum complications that keep me from working out."

In this case, please hold off on exercise and heed your doctor's orders for a healthy childbirth recovery. I've been there. The birth of my first daughter was so physically traumatic that I came away from it with a fourth-degree perineum tear and orders to refrain for ten solid weeks from any activity other than walking between my car and whatever place I was going. The first time I tried to run a few blocks, about three or four months post-childbirth, I had the distinct sensation that certain parts of my body were going to fall right out. Of course they didn't, but I *definitely* know what it's like to have postpartum complications derail your fitness regimen. Eventually I was able, little by very little, to work up to a normal exercise routine again—and so will you. Don't sweat it. (Literally.)

Fitness Solutions for Busy Stay-at-Home Moms

You didn't think I was going to let you get away with those excuses (other than the last one), did you?

Listen, I have experienced every single one of the above barriers to exercise, so not only do I empathize with any mom who is struggling with them, I have real-world solutions for how to overcome each one because I've done it. Since I'm no Superwoman, if I can do it, so can you. Here's how:

No time? Think small.

There are some endeavors in life that are either whole-hog or nothing at all; you're either in it with your entire being and your whole schedule or you sit this one out. Marathon-training and climbing Mount Everest come to mind. (Or, hey! Mothering!) The good news is that fitness is not one of those things. When it comes to exercise, or any type of physical activity, small chunks throughout the day add up to real benefits, and anything is better than nothing. In other words, you don't have to have an hour or more per day to exercise in order to get fitter, stronger, and leaner. Ten minutes here, ten minutes there, and ten more minutes in front of the TV at night add up to a perfectly respectable half-hour workout, and a very reasonable place to start.

So, if your time is crunched, consider the following ideas: commit to that ten minutes in the morning, ten minutes in the afternoon, and ten minutes in the evening, three times per week (or whatever frequency works for you—you can always add on!). Those ten minutes could be push-ups and ab crunches while your kids are napping, at preschool, watching a little children's TV, hanging out in the bouncy seat, baby swing, or ExerSaucer, or busy on someone else's knee. They could be jumping rope, or jogging in place on a mini-trampoline (or just on the floor if you don't own a trampoline). Climbing up and down a staircase in your home. Using an exercise DVD with short segments you can do individually if you don't have much time. Heck, one winter when my kids were babies and I couldn't leave the house or find any other way to exercise, I jogged laps around the first floor of my home while they napped—rounding the dining room table, loping through the kitchen, around the entry, and back through the living room, over and over and over. It was something!

Another idea is to combine exercise with other duties, effectively killing two birds with one stone. This way you use as little time as possible because you're also doing something else you'd have to do anyway. An example is putting the baby in a jogging stroller for a run, thereby giving her fresh air, outdoor stimulation, and maybe a gently rocking invitation to nap, all while you get your heart pumping. Or run errands on foot or on a bike with kids in tow (stroller, bike trailer, baby backpack) and get two things done at once.

Make school drop-offs or pick-ups your workout sessions. If you live close enough, run with an empty stroller up to preschool at pick-up time, and walk your toddler home in it once school lets out. Do the reverse for school drop-off. Let your older child bike to school while you jog alongside. Run laps around the outside perimeter of the field while watching your child's soccer practice.

One last idea is to make playtime your exercise time. Play hopscotch, tag, or soccer outside with your kids and count all that jumping, running, and kicking as workout time. Your children will love it, and you'll be amazed what a sweat you can work up playing games!

Energy begets energy.

So you feel tired and run-down. You feel like you have the energy of an obese housecat. That's okay, because as soon as you begin to exercise, your energy will increase. Really! It's one of those strange-but-true facts about the human body, kind of like how going out into bright sun can make you sneeze. Expend some energy, and you'll get more energy back. Which makes you feel better during your busy-mom day, and allows you to expend energy all over again to exercise again, which in turn gives you more energy. You see how it goes.

If the argument that energy begets energy doesn't rouse you out of your sleep-deprived stupor and drive you to go for a brisk walk or refreshing bike ride, consider tackling your no-energy obstacle by—again!—starting small, and adding time onto your workout sessions as you become stronger and less fatigued, or by changing the time of day you exercise. Maybe you have more energy at the break of day than you do at 7 p.m. Or, if you're like me, the idea of exercising at 6 a.m. makes you want to cry, so you give up on that notion, even if it works so well for your best friend, and you go running at dinnertime instead. Your husband and children can get by eating without you twice per week. Really. No one will be traumatized. I swear.

Everyone else feels fat, flabby, and out of shape too.

Or they used to. Or they will. Seriously, if some distorted sense of negative body image is what's keeping you from working out, you need to take some serious cognitive action. Remember that idea of reframing? When you restate something seemingly negative in positive terms, to affect your mood (and behavior) in a beneficial way? You need to reframe *I feel too fat and out of shape to exercise* to *If I start exercising today, I will be helping my awesome childbearing body heal and restore itself to its previous levels of awesomeness, so I can go forth and be even more awesome.* It also doesn't hurt to remind yourself that we've all been there, and no fellow mom is going to judge you. If you're still self-conscious, consider joining a fitness class or exercise group specifically for moms, such as a stroller exercise program.

Maybe childcare needs to be a little creative.

If you're like me, and don't have nearby extended family with whom to drop off your children now and then, you may need to rethink your idea of childcare in order to squeeze in some weekly exercise time.

One idea is to form a kid swap with another like-minded mama in need of some solo exercise time. Once a week, you leave your kids with her for an hour and go for a walk, run, or bike ride around her neighborhood, or zip over to the gym. Later in the week, you return the favor for her. The two of you can determine the schedule, frequency, and duration of these child swaps. The added plus with this arrangement is that your kiddos get a playdate out of it as well. Fun for all!

Another option is to utilize the childcare service at the gym. Affordable fitness centers, like YMCAs, usually offer free childcare along with their memberships, and it can be a boon for a busy mom who needs the security of knowing she's just a room away should things go awry. Also, gym childcare rooms are usually super-fun, with new activities for the kids and plenty of distracting diversions.

Don't forget the other ideas we've discussed here already: bringing your kid(s) along as you exercise and using naptime, "quiet time," or school time to squeeze in a workout. And finally, enlist your partner's help. You're in this parenting thing together, right? Figure out a schedule of childcare that works for the two of you and allows you time to take care of your physical health.

And if all else fails, you can always do your workout with your kids right there with you, underfoot, in the way, and providing sideline narration as you slog through the lunges and squats on your exercise DVD. After all, something is better than nothing, and sometimes children's unwitting hilarity can make a workout a heck of a lot more entertaining. As readers of *Mama in Wonderland* know, my daughters have often "participated" in my exercise sessions:

Excerpts from the running commentary that accompanied my workout this evening, as my four-and six-year-olds joined in while I did day five of Jillian Michaels 30-Day Shred:

"Why does that -teacher look mad?"

"My arms are already strong. How do you make your hands stronger?"

"This does not feel relaxing."

"When do we get to sit down?"

"Is this Friday Night Lights?"

Although I'm sure I did wish I were watching Friday Night Lights rather than performing exercises with such fear-inducing names as "traveling push-ups" and "jumping lunges" (ouch!), I can tell you that having my little girls there with me certainly made that particular workout a lot more fun.

Motivation can be manufactured.

As I said before, I've fallen victim to lack of exercise motivation plenty of times. Who hasn't? Fortunately, there are tons of tricks to up your fitness motivation. Surely one—or several!—of these will work for you.

Make a written list of reasons to exercise, and post it where you will see it every day. A visual reminder can be a powerful thing. It's harder to ignore a piece of paper on the refrigerator door that says, "Skinny jeans!!!" than some vague notion in your head that exercising might be a good idea. It also keeps front and center in your mind all the benefits of choosing a nightly walk over a nightly loungefest on the sofa.

Find a workout buddy. I've never done this myself, since, for me, exercising is a blissfully solitary pursuit, but I've heard many other women rave about this strategy for sticking to a workout plan. And it's easy to see why. Are you really going to blow off your fellow-mom running partner, who is likely all suited up and ready to go, waiting for you, because you just don't feel like exercising today? You don't need more guilt in your life, believe me. Make a pact, and then show up. Every time.

Make it even more social by starting a weekly moms' walking group. Truly, you could organize this around any fitness activity, but walking is probably the most egalitarian, suitable for the widest variety of exercisers. Plus it's inexpensive and you can talk while doing it. How fun is that?

Lay your workout clothes and shoes out ahead of time: the night before if you're an early-a.m. exerciser; when you're getting dressed for the day if you sneak something in during nap; or pre-dinner if you dash out the door for a workout when the kids go to bed. Sometimes just the thought of going to any sort of effort, even as minimal as pulling appropriate workout clothes out of a drawer, is enough to derail you. Get it all ready beforehand, then let those clothes lying on your bed all day give you the stink-eye if you so much as consider skipping out on your agreed-upon rendezvous.

Plan some rewards for after a particularly tough workout, a solid week of workouts, a mile run, ten times around the track, six months of BODYPUMP™ class at the gym—whatever increment seems challenging but doable. Rewards are the ultimate in motivation. Why do you think those rats get the food pellet every time they press the lever in all those biopsychology experiments? Don't go undoing all your hard work by having your reward be a giant bar of chocolate or bag of Cheetos, though. Pick something just as fantastic but a lot less caloric: a favorite TV show, a manicure, a great novel, a new athletic outfit. Consider it your food pellet.

Remind yourself that you are a role model for your children—doubtless the most important role model they have. If you want your kids to grow up fit and healthy and thinking of physical activity as a regular, required, but still fun, part of life, they need to see you engaging in it, starting now.

Speaking of your children, another way to combat low motivation is to make exercise—some of the time at least—a family event. This idea works best when your children are either babies (young enough to be toted, pulled, or pushed) or solidly school age (old enough to ride a bike without needing you to prod them up inclines, prevent nasty spills when they stop or try to turn around, or dash into the path of danger for them when they don't pay attention to that car backing out of its driveway). But with a little brainstorming, I bet you can think of at least a few ways you can work up a sweat and tone some muscles while also enjoying the satisfaction of knowing you've done something healthy and fun together as a family. A hike in a nearby nature preserve or state park? A bike ride to the playground? A walk along the river or in the woods? Ice skating? Sledding? Think of all those times walking back up the hill with the sled!

Lastly, consider making the occasional workout into a date night. If your spouse enjoys the same workouts you do, use your sitter not to go to a movie and dinner but to egg each other on for a five-mile run, then maybe go to dinner afterward. I'm not suggesting every date be a training run. But every now and then it might make those fitness goals a bit more fun to work on.

Money doesn't matter.

Exercise doesn't have to be expensive; in fact, it can be free. Playing kickball with your kids, walking, running, climbing the stairs in your house—these activities cost nothing more than, perhaps, a good pair of shoes. (And honestly, athletic shoes are not where you should skimp on price; seek advice at a specialty sports store and buy the best you can afford if you have a history of injury or orthopedic problems, a solid mid-range model if you don't. Your feet and joints are worth it.)

You don't need a membership at a high-end gym or a multi-thousand-dollar home-workout machine. You don't need fancy workout clothes, though a new outfit can be a great reward. Don't let a tight budget hold you back from getting fit. Start with what you have, even if that means hefting jugs of laundry detergent to perform bicep curls in lieu of the handheld weights you don't own and can't afford to buy. Turn on some music and dance with your preschooler. Go outside and run up and down that hill in your backyard. Grab a friend and walk around the neighborhood every night after dinner. Spend time and energy, not money (unless you have money you want and can afford to spend).

There's a time and a place.

If right now isn't your time to jump into a moms' fitness plan because you're a brand-new mom with childbirth-related injuries that need to heal, or other postpartum health reasons for taking it easy, cherish your time with your new baby and care for yourself as best you can to fully heal. Listen to your OB or midwife, take things slow, and know that there will be plenty of time to rock the fit-mama look later—the whole rest of your life, in fact.

Creating a Fit Lifestyle

First, a disclaimer: I'm neither a physician nor a certified personal trainer. To best ensure your own health and safety, you should consult your doctor for medical clearance before you begin a new fitness regimen—especially if you're newly or recently postpartum.

But though I'm not a fitness professional, I am a busy stay-at-home mom who's been a regular exerciser for more than 20 years, as well as a clinical health psychologist experienced in advising clients about the habits, including exercise, that affect physical health. This section contains all the basics you need to know to jump-start your own fitness program.

Wait—where's the Action Plan? For the purposes of guiding you through establishing a fitness regimen, I've chosen here to stray from the strict Weekly Goal/Daily Goal structure used in Chapter 3's Action Plan for self-care. That's because I believe fitness lends itself better to a more personalized, open-ended approach, one that you will determine as you go.

There's generally a real-world limit or some kind of expert-determined parameter for the hours of sleep you should get each night or the number of glasses of water your body requires. But when it comes to starting a novice fitness program, flexibility and freedom are especially important, because you're going to be figuring out what works specifically for you within an area that's highly individual. What you "should" do depends very much on your unique body type, lifestyle, and pre-existing health conditions. It may mean starting off with a 10-minute walk or a three-mile run; it may mean adding five minutes more each day or five minutes more each week. Allow for some fluidity, but stick to the following general guidelines.

Start with cardio. Cardiovascular, or aerobic, exercise is the activity that gets your heart pumping hard. It's also the exercise that burns the most calories and will most quickly blast away excess fat. Ultimately you should perform cardio exercise for 30 to 60 minutes, most days of the week, but that's an end goal, not a starting point. To begin, do what you can, even if that's limited to a 10-minute walk. Add five minutes every week, or as often as you feel able. Eventually you'll get up to that hour recommendation.

Below are some other examples of cardiovascular exercise. Pick something—or a few things—you enjoy. Exercise should be fun!

- ✓ Brisk walking
- ✓ Running
- ✓ Dancing
- ✓ Swimming
- ✓ Bicycling
- ✓ Stair-climbing
- ✓ Jumping rope
- ✓ Cross-country skiing
- ✓ Ice skating
- ✓ Elliptical-machine running
- ✓ Jumping on a mini-trampoline (Rebounding)
- ✓ Vigorous gardening (i.e. raking leaves, hauling debris, shoveling dirt)
- ✓ Shoveling snow
- ✓ Kickboxing
- ✓ Hiking
- ✓ Inline skating

Once you've got your cardio groove going, add strength training twice per week. This doesn't have to be super-time-consuming or anything complicated. But strength training is important, because it builds muscle mass. Muscle burns more calories than fat, and raises your overall metabolism, causing you to burn more calories all day, not just when you're working out. Plus, strength training contributes to strong bones.

To get started, collect some handheld free weights, resistance bands, or common household items you can use as weights (canned goods, filled water bottles, paint cans, handled laundry detergent jugs). Or, if you belong to a gym, sign up for a strength training class or book a session with a trainer who can instruct you on how to use the weight machines.

You'll want to work all the major muscle groups, performing one to three sets of eight to twelve repetitions of each exercise. Some common strength moves include:

- ✓ Bicep curls
- ✓ Triceps kickbacks
- ✓ Ab crunches
- ✓ Push-ups
- ✓ Squats
- ✓ Lunges
- ✓ Chest presses
- ✓ Dead lifts
- ✓ Shoulder raises

Examples of and instructions for various strength exercises can be easily found online, in fitness magazines, and as part of workout DVDs. Start small, especially if you've never lifted weights before, and experiment to find out which exercises you like best for each muscle group. Leave a day or two between each strength workout for muscle recovery.

You'll likely start noticing the benefits of strength training within a few weeks of consistent workouts: a more toned body, enhanced weight loss, greater energy, improved strength, and more stamina during your normal daily activities. And then there are all the benefits you can't see—the fortified bones; the reduced blood pressure, cholesterol, and risk of heart disease; the humming metabolism. Keep at it, and before long you'll be flexing that bicep and impressing your kids. Heck, maybe you'll even be able to bench-press them.

FIVE

MASTERING YOUR MOODS:

THEY'RE NOT THE BOSS OF YOU

BACK WHEN MY DAUGHTERS were two and four, I went through a period of stress so severe it made my hair fall out. In fact, that's how my girls still refer to it: "The Summer Genevieve Screamed All the Time and Mama's Hair Fell Out." Nice, right? They're too little to truly remember those months themselves, but for awhile, when it was still fresh, it was a frequent subject of family discussion.

Genevieve was in the throes of the Terrible Twos, and in addition to displaying all the usual daytime temper tantrums, she screamed at every bedtime and woke up crying multiple times overnight, every night. I had taken on a volunteer position at my daughter's nursery school that suddenly and unexpectedly turned into a nightmare of stress and time-suckage, but from which I could not extricate myself. I had no family support nearby, and no money to pay for a sitter. Life was really, really hard. This is what I sounded like back then on my blog:

This morning I went to the doctor to determine why my hair keeps falling out in chunks. I'm talking big, palm-sized chunks, every time I wash my hair. At this rate, I'll be bald by my 38th birthday. There's also the racing heartbeat, the cracked lips, the four-month-old rash around my mouth, and the fact that 90% of the time my body feels like someone accidentally flipped it into fifth gear and it's stuck there–that racing, revved feeling that won't go away no matter what you do, no matter how many bubble baths you take or five-mile runs you power through? That's a weird thing, people.

...It turns out that apparently all those symptoms are caused by STRESS. Which, you know, kinda goes both ways: GOOD NEWS! YOU'RE NOT SUFFERING FROM A SERIOUS ILLNESS WHICH MANIFESTS ITSELF IN YOU LOSING ALL YOUR HAIR! But then: HOWEVER! YOU'RE LOSING ALL YOUR HAIR!

Did I mention that my famously ultra-low blood pressure and pulse rates were elevated? Seriously, that NEVER happens to me. I could be birthing a baby over 60 hours of back labor and my blood pressure and pulse rates would still indicate that everything's cool. In fact, I think I did that once.

I went on to discuss, in some sort of mild hysteria, all the reasons for my stress and why I felt like I should be over it already, and something about prescription medication.

My point is, stress happens to *everyone*—even clinical health psychologists with specializations in women's health and mood management. If you're a stay-at-home mom, you will experience stress unlike any you've ever faced; it's pretty much a guarantee. Once you've full-time-parented two babies in diapers through a Minnesota winter with no family nearby and only occasional access to transportation, you look back at all those nerve-wracking PowerPoint presentations or 7 a.m. administrative meetings or difficult clients and think, *Ha! Piece of cake. Cake!*

Modern stay-at-home motherhood is especially stressful. Today, fewer of us have help in the form of local extended family. (Why yes, I *have* taken my child along to my gynecologist exam! How about you?) Many of us are super-mobile, moving from city to city more often than previous generations ever did, in pursuit of advanced degrees and sometimes-scarce career opportunities and potentially affordable housing. This leaves us more isolated than we otherwise might be, with fewer long-time friends and less intimate knowledge of the resources available to us in our communities. One income goes a lot less far than it once did, adding financial stress to our lives that can make us feel uncertain about giving up our salaries to raise children.

It's all a little much to deal with. Which may help explain why even the minor speed bumps of parenting can sometimes threaten to overwhelm us. For example, the year my older daughter started first grade, the intellectual challenges involved appeared to be mine as I became so overwhelmed while attempting to purchase her first school lunch box that immediately afterward I likened it to taking the SAT:

> *...Above the lunch boxes hang an entire wall of water bottles, Thermos containers, sandwich boxes, special ice packs, and lidded snack bowls. You become distracted by these accessories. How can so many school lunch items even exist? Which do you need? Is there some sort of guide somewhere? Why are there tons of Hello Kitty lunch box containers, but no Princesses ones to match*

the Princesses lunch box? You can't put a Hello Kitty water bottle into a Princesses lunch box. Or can you?????

...What are these metal Thermos-brand short cylindrical food containers? For keeping things hot? And/or cold? Do you need this? You don't know. You suppose so, if you are ever going to send anything for lunch besides a sandwich, which you probably will. But will you, really? Wait a minute: if you have an ice pack to keep the water bottle cold, will that cancel out the Thermos hot-food container's capabilities? This is confusing. Does all of this fit in the Princesses lunch box?

...Your children are whining that they are hungry and want to go home. Wondering what is taking you so long. They are beginning to rebel.

You buy the Princesses lunch box, the special ice pack, a water bottle, and a hot-food container. You make a mental note to save all receipts.

On the way out, you remark out loud that you feel like you just took an exam.

*Wow, first grade is **hard**!*

Thank goodness for social networking, because what started out as a minor mama freak-out turned into a fun blog conversation instead. As it turns out, I'm not the only mama who's been flummoxed by the school lunch box aisle. Writing about it helped me put it into perspective, and receiving immediate validation from others made me feel understood.

We've talked already, in previous chapters, about the importance of taking care of ourselves, in general. Then we talked in detail about one aspect of self-care: regular exercise. And while all those topics touched on mood and stress management, like exercise as a stress-reliever, and better sleep for better moods, the current chapter delves more deeply into the psychological, emotional struggles we all have at times, and in particular with the isolation that can accompany motherhood, and what we can do about it. Because stress and distress can be, *Oh my God, I forgot to bring snack for 20 preschoolers.* But it can also be, *If I don't get eight solid hours of sleep JUST ONCE this year, I may very well fake my own death and start a new life in rural Montana with little more than a big bed and maybe a cat.* One is just a wee bit more serious, wouldn't you say?

One fellow-mom friend of mine, when her daughters were toddlers, used to regularly fantasize about sneaking away to spend the night at a lovely, quiet hotel by herself—in her own town. If that doesn't speak to the world-shrinking desperation many a stay-at-home mom feels—the idea that a solitary getaway as attenuated as traveling *two miles across town* would seem like a pie-in-the-sky luxury—well, I don't know what does.

Most, if not all, of us have our moments of poor mental health, even if we're not clinically diagnosable. But here's where a serious caveat comes in. While I'm talking here about everyday stress and negative moods that can ruin your day (or your week) and perhaps lead you to dream of a night in a hotel room by yourself, more serious conditions exist too that are beyond the scope of this book.

Postpartum depression (PPD), postpartum anxiety, and other episodes of clinical depression and anxiety disorders are serious illnesses that require professional treatment—the sooner, the better. Although I am a clinical psychologist who has treated many patients over the years with these diagnoses, this book is not a treatment manual for mood disorders, nor is it meant to be a substitute for psychotherapeutic help. If you feel hopelessly sad or anxious, experience troubling physical or emotional symptoms that won't go away, or just have the nagging sense that you need help immediately, please call your obstetrician/gynecologist, primary care physician, or nurse practitioner—whoever provides your medical care—today, and ask for an appointment to discuss how you're feeling and the possibility of a psychotherapy referral and/or medication.

Most of all, if you *ever* experience urges to harm yourself or your child(ren), tell someone immediately, call 911 or a crisis hotline, or walk into a hospital Emergency Department and ask for help. Life is not supposed to be like that. There is help out there.

For now, let's assume you're not struggling with PPD or another clinical mood disorder, but instead are looking to improve your mood when necessary. So, what types of moods am I talking about here? What kinds of stress? And what do I mean by the two?

When I use the word "mood," I'm referring to a specific emotional state—the way you feel inside as you move through your hours. "Stress," however, is the external stuff out there in the world that we all deal with every day—the situations and circumstances linked to those internal moods. Moods are personal and internal; stress is the stuff of life. While there is a great deal of overlap in what works to ameliorate each, the solutions for negative moods tend to be more clinically-oriented and rooted in the principles of basic psychology; the solutions for stress lean toward the practical.

In my experience, it's not the least bit uncommon for stay-at-home moms to feel, at times, sad, overwhelmed, anxious, angry, frustrated, discouraged, and impatient. I, for one, know that I've experienced every one of these moods many times. Sometimes all in the same day. I'm not including the positive moods here.

Generally speaking, you don't need to "manage" those—just savor them.

And what about stress? Do we even need to name the numerous sources of stress in the modern mom's daily life? Shall we, anyway? Stress from the newness of parenting (see Chapter 1), sleep deprivation, worry over your children's well-being, a mile-long to-do list, the enormous responsibility of raising a child. Stress over endless parenting debates (breastfeeding or bottle? co-sleep or not? cry-it-out or attachment parenting? public or private school? sugar and the occasional preservative, or organics only?). Stress over not enough time for your friendships and not enough time for your marriage. Financial stress, career concerns, and the fact that each new developmental stage your child goes through brings new stress of its own.

Life isn't going to become stress-free anytime soon, and bad moods are inevitable at times. (A lot of times, if your child happens to be at that throw-herself-on-the-floor-at-Target-and-scream stage.) Which means that mood and stress management skills are not only handy, they're *necessary*.

The Mind-Body Connection

First, a little basic information about how moods and stress operate in your body. Moods are powerfully entangled with both biological processes and the thoughts swirling around in your mind. It starts with a thought about a situation, either conscious or under-the-radar, almost reflexive. That thought triggers emotion, thus setting your mood. Biological changes and physical sensations come next, and play a key role in how you feel, too—I'll explain more in a bit—but first, let's examine how your thoughts determine your feelings.

That's right: your thoughts come first. When I make that statement to my therapy clients, they look at me skeptically. I know it sounds counter-intuitive, so I'll give you the same example I give my clients. Imagine the difference in emotions you'd experience in this scenario: walking through the woods, hearing a rustling in the bushes nearby, and thinking, *Oh my God, a bear!* vs. this alternate scenario: walking through the woods, hearing a rustling in the bushes, and thinking, *What a nice breeze today, rustling the leaves and branches like that.*

In the first case, you'd likely experience intense fear and anxiety, whereas in the second, you'd feel content and complacent, perhaps even blissful. And yet the only difference in those two situations is the hypothetical thought that popped into your mind.

How we feel is influenced by what we think, like it or not, and that is a key tenet in a form of psychotherapy known as cognitive-behavioral therapy, or CBT. Now, you don't need therapy—or moods and stress severe enough to need therapy—to apply CBT strategies to your daily life, and to benefit from them. I'm going to teach you how in this chapter.

Once you've had the thought and generated the feeling, your emotions trigger a number of biological changes and processes: physical reactions to your emotions. For example, when you're in an anxiety-provoking situation, your body's level of the stress hormone cortisol shoots up, which causes rapid heartbeat, butterflies in your stomach, shallow breathing, and sweating. If you're in a situation that makes you feel sad, your physical energy wanes and you may feel nauseated or experience a lack of appetite. These are all physical sensations triggered by the onset of a feeling, which itself was triggered by a thought about a situation. The mind is a powerful thing, isn't it?

What's problematic, though, is the fact that our bodies respond to our moods in this way, *whether or not the thoughts that triggered the moods are accurate.* In other words, even if you totally misperceive and misjudge a situation, leading to a completely misguided thought about what's happening, your subsequent emotions and physical reactions will be exactly the same as if your assessment of your circumstances is correct. So, if your immediate thought about a stressor in your life is a negative, but inaccurate one (i.e., "This baby is never going to stop crying"), your subsequent mood—despair—is an unnecessary one. And who wants to experience bad moods unnecessarily?

An important note: I'm not saying these thoughts and negative moods aren't *understandable.* In fact, if you assessed your situation correctly, and your mood stinks because your situation stinks, the system is working for you. A troubled mood might be just the motivation you need to hunker down and work on some ongoing situation in your life that begs for a change. Still, a lot of us spend a whole lot of time feeling upset, stressed, discouraged, and angry at times when perhaps a more careful assessment of the triggering situation could spare us some misery. You can train yourself to have more discerning thoughts, thoughts that may lead to far more manageable moods.

Since it can be hard to view upsetting situations differently when you're already stuck in a cycle of negative mood, you can also *do* things to move yourself out of your bad mood through behavior. That's where the "behavioral" part of "cognitive–behavioral therapy" comes in. Many times, once you take action and get busy, you'll find yourself thinking and feeling better afterward. So we'll address both strategies here.

Remember, if you're a new mom, or if you're a nursing mom going through the weaning process, you are at the mercy of hormonal maelstroms about which there is little you can do. In the days immediately after birth and weaning, your hormones take you on a wild ride as they drop suddenly, often taking your mood with them. The best thing you can do during these times of transition is to educate yourself—and your spouse or partner—about these hormonal shifts and their effects, so you know what's going on when you suddenly burst into tears in front of the mailman for no apparent reason, or become inexplicably convinced that your house is not safe and proceed to tell your husband that you and he need to move as soon as possible (a personal, postpartum example). You may not be able to prevent these sudden, seemingly crazy emotions, but at least you can realize what's responsible for them. And you can know that these moods are temporary, which may be some consolation.

Skills and Strategies for Mood and Stress Management

While it's true that mood (internal, emotional, personal) and stress (external, circumstantial, the "stuff of life") are not the exact same psychological phenomenon, they often respond to the same interventions. In this section, I'm going to show you which CBT techniques work best for mood and stress management, and teach you how to apply them. I've added additional "stress-specific" advice at the end to address some unique aspects of coping with stress.

Cognitive-behavioral therapy techniques include strategies for tackling both your thought patterns (the "cognitive" part) and your behaviors (the "behavioral" part). That's because, while noticing and correcting unhelpful thoughts is crucial to managing negative moods, there are also times when you just feel too lousy to think logically even though it would be advantageous to do so. In those moments, targeting your physical behavior will allow you to calm down enough to then do the cognitive work necessary to set yourself straight.

Cognitive skills for managing moods and stress.

When you find yourself in a bad mood of any kind, there are several thought exercises you can take yourself through. Because remember: your bad mood could be based on erroneous thoughts, and therefore without basis in reality. And even if it's not, you can practice helpful self-talk that will make you feel a lot better.

Reframing.

This technique was introduced in Chapter 1. To remind you, reframing is restating a negative thought in a positive light. For example, maybe your current thought is: *our budget is so tight without me working, the financial strain is totally stressful!* Reframing the thought, you could tell yourself: *choosing this financial sacrifice is allowing me to be with my children full-time, which is a blessing I truly want.*

Correcting your thoughts.

Sometimes our thoughts are irrational and inaccurate. When you have a distressing, bad-mood-instigating thought, quickly check to see how true it is. If it's not 100% accurate, tell yourself the correct version. Example of an initial, reflexive thought: *we can't survive on one income like this. We'll* never be able to keep up with our bills! Corrected thought: it's not easy, but we have been surviving on one income. We've managed so far; we can keep it up.

Challenging your thoughts.

And what if your initial thought, even upon reflection, seems pretty accurate? Well, so what? Challenge yourself to consider what's the worst that could happen. For example, your initial, upsetting thought may be something like: I woke up sick as a dog so I'm not going to be able to help with that school event today, which will leave all the other volunteers short-handed all because of me. You then challenge that thought by saying, Well, so what? What does that mean? What's the worst that could happen? Which forces you to rebut your original panicky thought with something like: I might have to ask a friend if she can take my place today and I'll shoulder her turn next time. (And if your next panicky thought is: but what if no one else is free to do it? I'm still letting others down!, then you respond with the worst-case scenario rebuttal, which could be: well, all I can do is ask. The volunteer committee can't fault me for getting sick, and even if they're short a person, they'll be able to handle it.) When I walk my clients through this exercise in a therapy session, they almost universally come to the eventual conclusion that even the worst outcome is something they can handle.

Ask yourself the key question, "Next week / next year / in five years / when I'm 80, will this matter?"

Choose whichever time frame makes you feel best, and let the question put everything into perspective. Because I'll bet 95% of the time (at least!) the answer will be no.

Relatedly, remind yourself that if you won't care about whatever's bothering you next week (or whenever), why care now?

Save yourself the trouble and skip straight to the eventual mind-state. Ah, doesn't that feel better?

Remind yourself of your sources of social support.

No matter how distressing the situation, you're not in it alone. You have a partner, friends, family members, neighbors, health care professionals, counselors, your children's teachers, and this book to get you through.

Behavioral strategies for managing moods and stress.

When you're feeling lousy or stressed out, sometimes thought shifting isn't enough to flip the switch on your bad mood. That's why the actions you take are just as important.

Distract yourself.

Brooding rarely helps anything. When you're feeling angry, discouraged, down, anxious, or under stress, go watch a movie, read a magazine, or crack open a new juicy novel—anything to get your mind off whatever's bothering you for a while. It really helps. The caveat here to choose a healthy distraction strategy, and not the myriad unhealthy distractions that exist out there. I'm not talking about overeating, abusing alcohol, cigarette smoking or using illegal substances, or any other distraction that ultimately harms you rather than helps. Stick to the proactive, mind-engaging distractions in order to feel better

Talk it over with a sympathetic friend.

We all have those friends who are like balm to our raw moods, the go-to buddies we can count on to listen to our rants, tears, or fears, and then respond with exactly what we need to hear—namely, things like, "You're totally right here," "Everything's going to work out just fine," and "This too shall pass."

Exercise.

Physical activity is mood-enhancing. We've already spent an entire chapter talking about it, so I won't say more. But just know that scientific research has repeatedly demonstrated the mood-lifting powers of moving your body.

Treat yourself to something.

Especially when you've got babies in the house, it's easy to fall into a lifestyle that doesn't include much personal pleasure. After all, you're spending 24 hours a day meeting someone else's needs. Sometimes when you're feeling rotten, you just need a token of affection from you to you. It doesn't have to be big, or expensive. It just needs to lift your spirits a little.

Sleep!

Sleep deprivation is incredibly dysregulating. Although our culture assumes and promotes the idea that we can and should just power through if we're low on sleep, the biopsychological fact is that we need sleep to function normally and for our emotions to stay on an even keel. Of course, if you have a new baby in the house, or even a toddler or preschooler who doesn't reliably sleep through the night, you're not getting much sleep. Hence the irritability, despair, anxiety, and tendency to see the glass half empty rather than half full. It's only biologically logical. While it probably won't be possible to solve your sleep deficit, try as hard as you can to sleep whenever possible. Nap when the baby naps, go to bed as early as possible each night, ask for help from others. Get more sleep any way you can.

Get back to that favorite hobby or creative endeavor.

What soothes your soul or brings you bliss when you're doing it? Cooking? Gardening? Painting? Knitting? Baking? Writing? Walking? Reading? If you're feeling sad or upset, engage in that hobby for a bit and see how it helps your mood and your stress level.

Help someone else.

It's true what they say: helping others makes you feel better about your own situation. For one thing, helping another person takes your mind off yourself. It's a distraction. Then there's the positive social connection it brings, and the moment of feeling good about what you're doing. Helping others doesn't need to be especially time-consuming or grand in scale. Bring soup to a sick friend or share some extra home-baked cookies with your elderly neighbor. Help out at your child's school. Run an errand for someone.

Interrupting the stress response.

Now that you're familiar with the main cognitive and behavioral techniques to use for mood and stress management, I am going to give you some ideas for managing stress in particular. The experience of stress, while in some ways similar to negative moods like sadness or anger, carries its own particular swirl of symptoms. Stress reactions tend to perpetuate themselves: it's easy to get caught in a biophysiological feedback loop in which stress causes unpleasant physical symptoms, which make you more stressed, which leads to more symptoms, ad infinitum. Therefore, effective stress management includes a few ideas that go beyond the across-the-board strategies for feeling better as described above, and instead address the unique whirlwind of biological symptoms, such as racing heartbeat, rapid breathing, blood pressure spikes, and sweating, that make up the body's stress response.

When what you're feeling is more harried and hectic than sad or discouraged, consciously slow down your body and your actions, and remind yourself that "It's not an emergency." Because nine times out of ten, it's not. If you need stronger intervention to calm your body's stress reaction, try the following practical, effective stress reduction techniques.

Do some deep breathing.

Deep breathing exercises are stress management at its most basic. They're proven to help, and they have immediate impact on the distressing physical symptoms of stress (racing heartbeat, rapid breathing, blood pressure spikes, sweating, etc.). The simplest deep breathing exercise goes like this:

- *If possible, close your eyes.*

- *Take a slow, deep breath through your nose as you count to 4.*

- *Hold the breath for a second, and then exhale through your mouth, counting again to 4.*

- *Empty your lungs completely.*

- *Repeat, ideally for 10 to 15 minutes (but any duration is better than nothing).*

Take a yoga class.

There's a reason yoga has been espoused as a coping and relaxing practice across continents and for generations: it works. The meditative aspects of yoga help you see things more clearly, and practicing the poses burns off nervous energy. Give it a try, either with a local class, a DVD, or the help of a yogi friend.

Meditate or do another relaxation exercise.

Relaxation exercises have proven positive effects on the body and the mind. They can be as basic as sitting in a quiet room alone, with closed eyes, for 10 minutes every morning before beginning your day, focusing only on your breath or a comforting word such as "strength" or "calm." Or visualize the most relaxing scene you can imagine (a white-sand tropical beach? a wooded trail with snowflakes softly falling? the lake cabin where your family spent every summer while you were growing up?), and try to imagine it as vividly as you can, putting yourself in the scene, for 10 or 15 minutes.

Attend to your physical health.

You've (presumably) read Chapters 2 and 3 about self-care, so I'll keep this brief: proper vitamins, adequate hydration, enough sleep, physical exercise, and good nutrition go a long way in helping you manage daily stresses. Are you paying enough attention to your physical needs?

After all that, if nothing seems to be doing the trick to help you feel better when you're distressed, calmer when you're stressed, and generally just able to enjoy most of your daily life as a stay-at-home mom, do not hesitate to take mood and stress management a step further and seek psychotherapy and/or treatment with medication. Your OB, primary care physician, or nurse practitioner can help you determine which is right for you, how to start, and where to go from there.

We all get crabby, down, upset, and stressed; it's part of life. By practicing the strategies outlined in this chapter, you'll spend less time upset and stressed and more time enjoying motherhood.

SIX

BUILDING YOUR TRIBE

AWHILE BACK, I went through a pretty rough year—a really, really bad year, actually. My aging parents were having health issues, my toddler rebelled at every bedtime and still wasn't sleeping through the night, we'd lost more than half our retirement savings in the market crash, and my husband was (temporarily, it turned out) laid off from his second job—the part-time extra work that paid the bills that his day-job salary didn't quite cover.

My marriage was suffering, everything in my house was breaking, and my extended family was inaccessible. I had zero help with my children, ever, and the grind was really getting me down. I had no plan for my on-hiatus career, and no vision for how I would ever be able to earn money again. I suffered from crushing insomnia. My husband thought I had it easy all day, because for a few hours a week both children were in school for the first time. I thought that three hours a week—during which I frantically cleaned, cooked, ran errands, did the shopping, washed clothes, tried to write, and occasionally exercised—didn't exactly constitute "having it easy." He was unsupportive, I was demoralized and furious, and so we fought a lot. I was broke, tired, and at the end of my mothering rope. What I wasn't, though, was alone.

My friends got me through. And this is some of what I wrote to them on my blog that New Year's Eve:

> ...There were a lot of times this past year when I thought I might just crumble into a weepy pile of mothering housewifely nerves, save for the friendship and love of some pretty amazing people. And I just want to formally thank them all for helping me get through the last 12 months with my sanity (mostly) intact and my pulse (relatively) normal. Some are fellow moms I talk to nearly every day and who help me through the nitty-gritty of daily parenting, some are friends I rarely see in real life but who unfailingly stand behind me in everything I do and leave supportive comments and blogging-love for me via the Internet on a regular basis. One is a long-ago friend who tracked me down after 25 years, looked me up, and for some reason cared enough to read me, write me, and send me care packages through the mail; one is an Internet friend-of-a-friend who I have never even met in real life but who has sent me late-night and early-morning Facebook messages saying things like, "You are right" and "You can do it" and "I have felt that exact same way" at times when I could have cried with gratitude for such words. Sometimes I actually did. And, amazingly, some of the biggest and best supporters in my stay-at-home mom life are women who have never been mothers and yet feel like-surely are-friends to the end.

I know people say it takes a village to raise a child, but I don't know so much about that. What I know is that it takes a village to raise a *mother*. Every mom needs a solid tribe of friends at her back; they're what make stay-at-home motherhood doable, livable, and just plain fun. They're the ones who will lend you an extra diaper at the playground when you're caught unprepared, trade preschool parent-teacher conference times with you so you can make your dentist appointment, and provide the necessary gallows humor when head lice makes an appearance in your family for the first time. Plus, there are always going to be those graver times—times of true challenge and strife—when you can honestly say, "My life would suck without you."

I've always liked the concept of one's various friends as a "tribe," with its implied warrior-level loyalty and suggestion of a wide band of supporters—to the right, to the left, in front of, behind, near and far; wherever you look, there's your tribe. Think of your tribe as all the people you consider friends: some soul-sisters, some casual buddies, some in certain settings and some in others, some a mile away and some across the country or the world, a vast support-network of people who like you and want you to succeed.

Some of us are, by nature, introverts, and may wonder why one needs a tribe. Why not one or two close friends and that's that? And I hear you, because that was me once too. But what I've found as a stay-at-home mom is that sometimes what you desperately need isn't one or two close friends, it's another mom with a child in your daughter's class, who can pick up your child in the afternoon on short notice because you're still sitting in the exam room of an overscheduled orthopedist, 45 minutes behind schedule, with school letting out in half an hour.

A tribe gives you support, friendship, fun, perspective, love, help, encouragement, and home-baked brownies on your birthday (surely somebody does that for you). Your tribe gives you peace of mind at times, and vital information at times, and the latest scoop on clearance-priced 5T clothes, and the best class schedule for toddler gymnastics. A tribe will take in your mail when you're out of town or send you a jokey e-mail from 1,500 miles away when you really need a laugh.

In other words, a tribe is a collection of different beloved people, each serving her (or his) own important role in your life, just as you do in theirs. And once you have a tribe, you realize just how invaluable it is. (Some or all of the "she" pronouns in this section might be "he" for you. Go ahead and make that substitution in your head as you read, if so, and count yourself lucky; opposite-sex friendships can provide a different, valuable perspective on parenting—and everything else too.)

If you don't have a solid tribe yet, it's time to start building one. Here are some key tribe members to consider.

Tribe Members You Really Need

Your best local friend.

This is your closest friend in your own town, maybe even your own neighborhood, though not necessarily. She's a fellow mom, ideally with children in the same school(s) as yours. It's even better if her kids are the same age and/or gender as yours and like to play together, and if your husbands or partners like each other too; if you're lucky enough to get all that, you become each other's go-to family.

You have shared values, both in parenting and in other areas. You have similar family rules and don't need to explain to each other why you don't buy the DayGlo multi-colored Goldfish crackers or why you insist on a 7 p.m. bedtime even when the other neighborhood kids are still playing outside at that hour.

This is the friend you can call late at night in a panic over your toddler's croupy-sounding cough, or early in the morning with news that your dad just had a stroke. She's also the friend with whom you share hundreds of casual park playdates, field trips to the zoo, and those ten pounds of potatoes you bought at the grocery because it was buy five pounds, get five pounds free, only you can't use ten pounds of potatoes before they go bad. You love this friend like a sister, and her kids are like your own. You feel you'd never survive your daily mothering life without her.

Your best non-local friend.

This is the friend you've moved away from, or who has moved away from you, yet you remain in touch because you're connected in motherhood, and even distance can't erase your friendship. She may be an hour's drive away or halfway across the country; she may be a working mom or not; she may have one child or five. Maybe you met her in birthing class or at a former job or at the park when you were both postpartum with sleeping infants in strollers. Maybe she used to be your next-door neighbor.

A non-local friend is great for worry, and for venting about the stresses and strains of parenting and life, since nothing you say to her will come back to haunt you with the other moms in your town. She's far away; she doesn't know the mom at your child's elementary school who never answers e-mails or whose kid is wild. You can whine, joke, and snark to her about anything, and her distance helps her keep your secret—and adds an objective opinion to your daily dilemmas. You fervently thank the universe for Facebook, e-mail, and/or text messages every time you think of this friend. She may not be able to feed your cat when you travel to Grandma and Grandpa's for the holidays, or take your place at the PTA meeting when you wake up sick, but she's still got your back. You know that if you ever truly need her, she's only a phone call or status update away.

Your longest-time friend.

There's something comforting about having a friend who's known you forever, pre-kids or maybe even pre-adulthood. This may be the buddy you went to high-school football games with, or the friend who walked across the stage with you at graduate-school graduation. Her existence reminds you who you are and where you came from, which can be humbling or uplifting, depending on the circumstances.

This friend is great for laughs. For who but a long-time friend can impersonate that ridiculous professor you both had in college? Or remind you about the time the two of you and your husbands spent Thanksgiving together, stranded far from family as young married couples, and ate Chinese food and double-chocolate Ghirardelli brownies with a side of Stove Top stuffing?

The best thing about this friend is that, by nature of the fact that you're still friends after all these years, she really loves you, which means that in times of crisis or even just a particularly rough patch, she will be there for you. Even if she hasn't seen your face in person or held your hand in a dozen years, you both know that your bond still exists. It's the sort of thing that helps a person sleep at night.

Your childless friend.

Gasp! Can you still be friends with someone once you've become a mother, and **she** hasn't? Sure, and it can be extremely valuable.

Let's face it, we parents are an insular group, who tend to suffer the inevitable myopia that comes with having babies and then suddenly being responsible for another human being. We can talk for hours about the merits of different types of strollers (and we're genuinely concerned about it!). We can—and, sorry! often do—agonize over things like when to introduce solids and how best to handle separation anxiety and whether the artsy charter school with the long waiting list is better than the local neighborhood school. We start to think that the sun rises and sets on the ups and downs of our children's sleep habits. We do things like chart their potty training progress with Dora the Explorer stickers.

In other words, most of us need a reality check now and then, a connection to the "outside world" of adult life, a fresh set of eyes upon our latest parenting problem—a set that doesn't belong to another parent and therefore may sometimes lead to a different, helpful perspective.

If our childless friends can stand us, we benefit from their different sort of sympathy during our hard mothering times, their more detached problem-solving, and the fact that their differing daily experiences provide us with vicarious entertainment that doesn't have a thing to do with small children.

Your neighbor.

I've experienced time and again how awesome it is to have a great neighbor or two in your tribe. A neighbor is as local a tribe member as you can get. She is great for all manner of emergencies, including bringing you Pedialyte and saltines when you're trapped at home with a vomiting five-year-old and nothing stomach-flu-friendly on hand, bus stop coverage when you realize you need to be bringing one child to the pediatrician at the same time you're supposed to be waiting for the school bus with the other, carpool-sharing if your kids go to school together, and ideas for good nearby babysitters.

Your fellow-school mom friend.

This friend doesn't have to be your closest confidante or go-to playdate mom, though she could be. She's someone you like and are friendly with, whose children go to the same school and are in the same grades as yours. This is the friend who can help you decipher school information and policies, volunteer with you at your kids' classroom Halloween party, hang out in the pick-up line with you and shoot the breeze. She can help with transportation emergencies, since she's going the same place you are each day, and you have the opportunity for potential after-school playdates together. Your friendship with her may even help your child make friends at school, since your kids already have a connection with one another through the two of you.

Your playgroup mom friends.

These were hands-down my most important friends during my early years of mothering. A new friend in a toddler-and-parent early-childhood class with me, a likewise mom to a 1-1/2-year-old and pregnant with baby number two, approached me about starting a playgroup shortly after I moved to my family's current hometown. She knew two other moms of 1-1/2-year-olds, also pregnant with their second babies, besides her and me, and thought the four of us would make a great similarly-circumstanced group.

We did—we are—and those three playgroup mom friends became the core of my local tribe, friends I saw regularly and shared countless playdates, conversations, parties, and parenting classes with.

For the most part, our children now attend different schools, and regular playgroup meetings have long lapsed, but we still get together occasionally and they will always be dear to my heart, because they met me at my loneliest, have seen me at my most exhausted, harried, and unkempt, and have provided a whole lot of fun over the years. Most important of all, I will always feel that they love my children, even if we haven't played together in months or years, because they knew them as babies and watched them grow.

If you join (or form!) a playgroup when one or more of your children are babies, you can have all that too, and those friends will stick with you long after the babies become big kids.

Your online tribe.

I'm not exaggerating at all when I say that some of my strongest supporters and key sources of comfort and commiseration—not to mention entertainment and laughs—are women with whom my only communication has been Internet-based and electronically-sent. Through writing my blog and reading others, I've established connections that have honestly changed my life in the way that vital friendships can. You don't need to meet someone in person for her to count as a dear friend, I've learned.

With your online friends, as with your non-local "in real life" friends, you have the invaluable luxury of knowing that they are far away and thus don't interact with your day-to-day circle of friends and relations. This makes them the perfect confidantes.

But an online tribe has some unique attributes as well. For one thing, your lives are not wrapped up with one another to the same degree as they generally are with in-person friendships. This means that you can enjoy and benefit from the one or two topics you may have deeply in common—mothering, for example, or crafting—while not worrying if other parts of your lives are wildly divergent—say, she's a Republican and you're a Democrat—which could lead to strife if she were a local friend, and you had reason and opportunity to discuss more than just your common blogging interests.

For another thing, you do not need to worry about whether or not you're devoting enough time to this friendship. Online communication tends to be quick, dashed off; you can respond to one moment in time and then log off without wondering if you should be scheduling a coffee date to catch up. These are fantastic, two-way-street, drop-in friendships that can either build up to stronger, longer-term relationships, or continue to pop sweetly in and out of the landscape of your social-networking life.

Of course you may not be as online-involved as I am, which is fine; but keep in mind that friends are everywhere—even four states away and across a fiber optic line.

Tribe Members to Avoid

Now that we've reviewed the most valuable members in your tribe of friends, let's say a quick word about types of friends (or should I say "friends") to avoid. These women aren't part of your tribe; they're incompatible with you for various reasons, even if you don't realize it right away. Basically, stay away, or extricate yourself as soon as possible, from "friends" who are:

Competitive.

Because honestly: who needs to run any more races in life?

Unsympathetic about your new responsibilities as a mom.

If you have a childless friend who won't cut you any slack at all in the "I'm a mom now, my life is different" arena, cut her loose.

Widely divergent from you in terms of personal values.

Sure, you can agree to disagree about some things with a friend; but if you find yourself viewing her entire lifestyle and world-view with distaste, it's time to move on.

Superior.

If she needs to feel better than you, she's not a tribe member. Enough said.

Unwilling to return a favor.

I'm not saying every little thing has to be tit for tat. In mothering life that would never fly. There will always be times when you need more from a friend at the moment, and other times when she needs more from you; in a solid friendship, this evens out over time. But if you're friends with someone who consistently takes without ever providing anything at all in return, question whether she would ever truly be there for you in a time of need.

Unsupportive.

Listen, a friend is supportive. She may not agree with everything you do 100% of the time, but she supports your emotions, your health, your well-being, your role as a mom, your right to make your own decisions, your core self. If someone in your life doesn't do any of that, she doesn't belong in your tribe of friends.

A caveat about all this friend business: remember that your needs and your friends' roles will change over time, as the years pass and your kids grow older. That's okay. What you need in a friend—who you need in your tribe—when you're newly postpartum with your first baby or parenting two toddlers under three or sending a child off to preschool is different from what you need in a friend when your children are in Little League or entering middle school or learning to drive. Don't worry about this; it's normal and expected. Things change. Friends change. Even tribes change.

———

The bottom line is, we all need a lot of different types of friends in our tribes. Mothering is hard; stay-at-home mothering can be isolating. We need as many people as possible to have our backs. And remember: what they do for you, you do for them, so be a good tribe member yourself. Everyone benefits when moms are happy, social, connected, safe, and sane. Even (especially!) our kids.

SEVEN

A QUICK AND DIRTY GUIDE
TO KEEPING YOUR
HOUSE CLEAN

IF YOU DISLIKE CLEANING as much as I do, you'll be happy
to know that this chapter is going to be short, quick, and
focused, just like the housecleaning plan it describes. Because as
far as I'm concerned, the less time talking about cleaning—let
alone doing it—the better. Of course, if you happen to love
cleaning, you'll find this chapter wholly unsatisfying. To you I
say: skip forward. And also: you are a better person than I.

Some of you fellow stay-at-home moms may not include
keeping house as part of your full-time job, but instead choose to
focus on parenting duties and share the housework with your
partners, after-hours. To you I say: fantastic! And also: *lucky you*.
However, in my family, my husband and I agree that keeping
house is part of my job as an at-home mom, and I know that
many at-home moms manage the bulk of the housekeeping for
their families as well.

My husband does the dinner dishes, unloads the dishwasher (usually) in the morning, and folds the laundry, but, for the most part, I do everything else—and there's a lot of "everything else." This works for us right now, but it has taken some time, growth, and trial and error on my part to find a system that allows me to parent successfully, get out of the house and enjoy my life, and also keep my house—and my sanity!—appropriately maintained.

Believe me, there *is* a way to keep your house clean and your tasks done without devoting your entire day to the drudgery of housework, even when your schedule is tight and your tasks are interrupted by school runs or a baby's cries. And once you've got a smoothly running system in place, it frees you up to be more social and spontaneous with your life and your household, and to fully enjoy the scarce down-time you do have by relaxing in a serene, clean environment rather than stressing out over the dust balls in the corner and the crumbs on the carpet. (Well, let's be honest: sometimes there are still going to be crumbs on the carpet, which is okay.)

My basic strategy is simple and old-fashioned. What it boils down to is this: I dislike cleaning so much that it is far more distasteful to me to have to spend a whole day or weekend cleaning an entire messy house than it is to do a little cleaning every day, according to a set schedule. The idea of utilizing a cleaning schedule is an easy way to take the thinking and procrastination out of household work and instead make it focused, quick, and reliably done.

The main element in this strategy is a list—written at first, until it becomes ingrained in your head, and then maybe just a mental schedule after that. My cleaning checklist began on a white-board attached to the refrigerator door. Post yours anyplace you'll see it regularly. The trick is to keep your schedule visible and salient, until it becomes a habit. I guarantee this will make a huge difference in your daily at-home mom life.

But wait. For those of you who are right now shaking your head in dismay and thinking to yourself that only a control freak would expect herself to turn a frenzied-mama existence into something resembling a college course syllabus, I ask you to reconsider. While on the surface, cleaning on a schedule may seem compulsive or fanatical, in actuality it is exactly the opposite: it reduces an overwhelming job (keeping the entire house clean) to daily, short tasks that together add up to a regular weekly cleaning.

I love my schedule, because I love knowing at the end of each week that my house actually got cleaned (mostly) top to bottom. And I think you will, too. Every job has its unpleasant duties. Housekeeping on a schedule at least makes cleaning house straightforward.

Before we get to the details of a housecleaning schedule, a few caveats for those of you whose primary reaction to this idea is an overwhelming urge to lie down for a nap. The truth is, I didn't clean like this (or this much) when I was pregnant, or when I worked part-time at night in addition to being home full-time with a baby during the days, or when I had newborns. I didn't clean like this when I had two toddlers in the house, or when both my girls were in diapers, or when my nights were still interrupted by nursing sessions. Want proof? Here's what I had to say on my blog about (not) cleaning my house when I had a newborn and a toddler at home—that's two babies in diapers, folks:

> *So, I realized today that, since having my second baby, I don't really clean anymore. Do laundry, yes, almost daily. Cook, naturally. Clean when company is coming*

to stay over? Yes. But actually engage in housecleaning chores for the general upkeep of our home? Like dust, scrub the kitchen counters/appliances, clean the toilets, tubs, and vanities, Swiff the floors? Oh my god, mop??? On anything resembling a regular basis--that is, with the frequency I used to do such things when I only had Julia to take care of? Um, no.

No, no, no, no, no.

This realization came to me because I was at playgroup with two other mom friends, and the conversation turned to that Holy Grail, the simultaneous nap. You know, when BOTH babies are napping at the SAME TIME. The other two moms were comparing notes on their respective systems for getting the bathrooms cleaned when this fabulous occurrence takes place.

Well, people, both of my babies are napping right now (after a particularly hellish post-playgroup lunch at home, involving all manner of meltdown and tantrum over things like the wrong color sippy cup, the spilled water from the sippy cup, the chicken touching the rice, etc. etc. etc., and ending with both babies screaming, water all over the table, chair, and floor, and a spoonful of cheesy broccoli flung onto the carpet. But that's another story. Right?), and guess what I am doing? Not scrubbing my toilets, I'll tell you that much. And I'll tell you something else. When my babies are both napping, I NEVER scrub the toilets. Okay? Never.

Back then, I sort of worried I may never become an organized housecleaner again. But, little by little, I did.

This has been an ongoing process, coming to this weekly system. If you're not quite at the point of instituting a structured system of keeping house, one day you will be. And by taking a few moments to envision how such a system would work, you're setting the foundation for how your life can look in three months, or six months, or a year, when you've entered the next phase of at-home motherhood and are ready to master the demands of children and household maintenance at the same time.

One other note about my cleaning schedule: this is quick cleaning. One reason I can clean quite quickly is that I keep the house fairly uncluttered; that makes it easier to speedily wipe down a kitchen counter or dust a dresser. I do these jobs thoroughly, yes, because it's a lot easier to keep things up than to let them slide and then have to clean an inch-thick swath of grime from the floor behind the toilet months down the road. But I can be thorough *and* fast; I have to, I have kids hanging off me most of the time—just like you.

What exactly does this schedule strategy entail? It's all about having an unvarying set of chores to accomplish each day of the week. You may choose, as I usually do, to leave weekend days free for family time, alone time, and relaxation. (At-home moms need regular time off too; see previous chapters!) By the end of the week, all main household cleaning tasks have been accomplished, and you have the satisfaction of knowing your entire house has been cleaned. Even better, because you're doing a little every day, your house is always in a state of relative cleanliness, and you'll never find yourself embarrassed to have a neighbor drop by unannounced again. You're on top of things; the house is mostly clean, most of the time—and all this in a fairly short period of time each day. What could be more satisfying?

What follows is an example of a weekly cleaning schedule—mine, actually. To this weekly schedule, you will add the tasks you need to do every day: the laundry, the cooking, the dishes, the cleaning of the cat box, the picking up of toys, or whatever meets your household needs. And remember, this weekly schedule is just one example. You may choose to move chores around to other days of the week. What matters is not which day you do what, but that each major cleaning job gets done each week, and no one day becomes completely consumed with an overwhelming number of chores. Take a look:

Monday: Clean the kitchen. (Scrub the sink; wipe down counters, appliances, and cabinets with disinfectant or soapy water.)

Tuesday: Dust all rooms. (I break this up into: dust main level; dust upstairs.) Shake out the rugs. Sweep or dust-mop all hard floors. (Wet-mop if needed.)

Wednesday: Vacuum all carpet. (I break this task up into: vacuum main level; vacuum the upholstered furniture; vacuum the stairs; vacuum the upstairs.)

Thursday: Clean bathrooms. (The usual: scrub sinks, vanities, toilets, tubs, and showers. Shine mirrors. Wipe down the baseboards, the bases of the toilets, and the floor around and behind the toilets.)

Friday: Water the plants. Empty all the trash cans. Put out fresh towels everywhere. Change the bed linens (though I confess I do not do this every week.)

I challenge you: try cleaning on a schedule for one month—those of you past the I-never-clean-the-bathrooms-during-naptime phase, I mean—and see if you don't love the structure and, paradoxically, the freedom it gives you.

EIGHT

LIVING A ONE-INCOME LIFE
IN A TWO-INCOME WORLD

HAVE YOU EVER NOTICED that people rarely talk about money? About the terrible economy and the recession and bank bailouts and Wall Street? Sure. About clearance sales and when those killer tall boots get marked down 40%? Definitely. But when it comes to sitting down and frankly discussing take-home salaries and how much you paid for your house and whether you're middle-class or not, and why? Not so much. In a lot of ways, money is as taboo a conversation topic as sex—maybe even more so. And how many of you are sitting around discussing your sex lives these days? I thought so. (Or, rather—I thought not.)

Nope, we hardly ever discuss income and money, and that can make all of us—each in her own individual financial circumstance, unbeknownst to everyone else—feel very alone. It's too bad, too, because most of us could use some helpful money-wise tips. I've learned quite a few over my seven years at home living on (mostly) just one income, and I'm sure other at-home moms have too.

The truth is, the reality of having or not having enough money becomes a lot more salient for most of us when we become stay-at-home moms. It's not easy in today's society for a dual-income couple to willingly give up an entire salary; in fact, it's such a stretch that these days it often *seems* that the only moms able to stay home with their kids are those with high-earning spouses. But is that really the case?

Back when my older daughter was one and I was pregnant with my second child, preparing to close down the part-time solo private practice I had maintained since quitting my full-time job when I became a mom, I wrote an essay about choosing stay-at-home motherhood despite my decidedly non-upper-class status (some might even have said lower-middle-class status). That essay generated a fair amount of buzz. Why? Because I had the gall to assert that "being able" to choose at-home motherhood isn't always about being lucky enough to be married to a doctor or an attorney or a high-level executive of a successful company.

I noted that some of us—for instance, me—chose stay-at-home motherhood even when doing so meant sharing one car between two adults, living in a tiny, shabby starter house in a sketchy neighborhood because it was all we could afford, dressing our children mainly in thrifted and hand-me-down baby clothes, giving up all travel beyond the occasional road trip to visit grandparents, forgoing cable TV and the latest large-screen TV and vacations to Disney and a new minivan and private school and organic milk and expensive admissions to museums and the zoo.

I explained that I wasn't a stay-at-home mom just because I was lucky—which, when voiced to me by envious working moms who had made different lifestyle choices, carried the implication that they just weren't lucky—but because my husband and I *made a lot of financial and material sacrifices to make it possible*. Not everyone got that, or was prepared to hear it. Of course there is another group of families for whom stay-at-home parenthood is truly out of reach, because neither parent makes a subsistence-level wage that can support a family, no matter how many sacrifices are made. I surely appreciate the blessing of having the option of at-home motherhood.

For many of us—not all, but many—living a one-income life in a two-income world is hard. Really hard. But that doesn't mean it's not worth it. It can be helpful during some of the hard times to think about how and why you made the decision to give up one income to become a stay-at-home mom in the first place. Time with your babies, surely. Deeply held values about parent-only care? Maybe your career was incompatible with parenting young children? Maybe you got laid off during your pregnancy and decided not to look for something new just yet? To reduce the (non-financial) stress and busyness in your daily life? So that you could exclusively breastfeed longer, something hard to do while working full-time? Because you missed your baby too much otherwise? Because your spouse wanted you to, and you were willing to give it a try? Because your child had birth complications or special needs or an illness that required significant care?

There are a multitude of reasons, all of them valid. You know your own reasons. You know they are more powerful than the figure on your last paycheck. But if you're like me, you also know that life on one income is a whole lot easier with a little stretch-your-dollar savvy. So read on!

Tips for One-Income Survival

Some of the following ideas for making a one-income life more livable may be new to you, and some may not. All are strategies I've learned in my years as an at-home mom, and, for the most part, are ones I live by daily. Pick and choose the ones that seem right for you, and don't be afraid to try out some that don't resonate at first glance. You never know what might become your surprise go-to money saver.

Avoid comparisons with other families' lifestyles, possessions, and financial situations.

This can be incredibly challenging, I admit. I am guilty of gazing up the hill at the million-dollar mansions in my neighborhood from the vantage point of my modest, edge-of-the-neighborhood townhouse and burning with the occasional ball of envy. Who wouldn't love granite countertops and a double oven in the kitchen, a giant yard for the children (plus money to afford to hire out the lawn care), and regular exotic vacations? But mamas, be warned: this kind of comparing will slowly eat away at you. Remind yourself that you have no idea how unhappy, unstable, or financially in over their heads those families might be, and move on.

Relatedly, hang out with likeminded and similarly-circumstanced friends and families.

You'll feel a lot more content with your one-income lifestyle if your family's best friends' houses, cars, clothes, activities, and values look a whole lot like yours.

Avoid catalogs and shopping malls.

It's amazing how much you don't know you "need" if you never see it in the first place. (Come to think of it, this applies to children's toy commercials and your kids, too. Another reason to limit TV time!)

Be merciless with the household budget.

Think about, or formally track, everything you spend money on, and then consider what you can do without. Don't think about such denial as permanent; focus on the here and now. In fact, don't think of it as denial at all. Think of it as trimming the fat to support your life as a full-time at-home mom. Some things to consider giving up: cable TV, salon manicures/pedicures (you can do them at home for free), travel, your cleaning service (if you have one), magazine or newspaper subscriptions (you can always get your news from the Internet), pricey coffee drinks, soda/juices/sports drinks (water is free, and healthier to boot), some of your children's expensive classes/lessons/activities (they don't need all of that anyway, truly), your gym membership (if you have one), eating out as much as you are used to. Larger sacrifices to consider include your family's second car, your land line (rely on your cell instead), and private school for your kids.

Focus on free socializing and recreation.

Use parks and playdates for fun rather than movies, museums, and other activities that cost money. (More specific recommendations follow.)

Use the library as entertainment.

Most public libraries offer free children's storytimes, and some offer many other free kids' events and activities as well.

Plus, of course, there are all those books, movies, and CDs to check out. Movie Night has never been so affordable!

Make date night an at-home event instead of an expensive night out.

Once the kids are asleep, you can curl up on the sofa with your sweetie, a glass of wine, and a movie on DVD—with no sitter expense.

Consider a buying ban.

Aside from the necessities of groceries, diapers, medicine, toilet paper, and the like, can you take a break from buying for the immediate future? How long can you go without spending money on non-necessities? A week? A month? Longer? Try it and see how long you can go.

Space out haircuts—if not your own, then at least your children's.

If their cuts don't involve bangs or layers, you can easily let them go long now and then with limited unkemptness.

Buy fewer processed and/or pre-packaged foods, especially snack foods.

We all know that cooking from scratch, buying in bulk and divvying up into smaller portions yourself, and eating whole foods more often than, say, Teddy Grahams, is cheaper. Don't let packages of pre-cut veggies or individual applesauce cups separate you from your household's money.

Give up household cleaners in favor of vinegar and baking soda.

Those bottles of sprays, foams, and scrubs are expensive! When my family was at its scrappiest, income-wise, I stopped buying commercial cleaners and instead filled an empty plastic spray bottle with half water, half white vinegar. I used it to clean every surface in the house, with baking soda as the occasional scrub for sinks and tubs. I've never looked back, and I'm amazed at the money I've saved.

Do a child swap rather than pay a babysitter.

Sitters can be expensive. Join forces with close friends and take turns watching each other's kids while the free couple goes out for an afternoon or evening. Your kids can play together, and you get free babysitting.

Free day at the museum.

Enough said!

Likewise: discount hours at the city pool.

In my town, that's after five every night, when most little swimmers go home for dinner, bath, and bed.

Determine an alternate plan with relatives for holiday gifts.

Depending on the size of your extended family, gift giving can put a major dent in your household budget. Who knows, maybe your siblings, aunts, and uncles are looking to cut down on holiday spending as well. Consider drawing names, giving family gifts (a board game, a zoo pass) rather than a present for each family member, or presents for kiddos only.

When you're cooking, use every scrap.

If you don't know how to do this, learn. Veggie scraps can be used for stock, soups, stews, and frittatas. Leftover juice from drained canned tomatoes can be used in soup, chili, and pasta. On-the-verge-of-sour milk is great in pancake and muffin batter. (What do you think buttermilk is?) Stale bread can be cubed for croutons, processed for bread crumbs, or toasted for garlic bread. Stop throwing groceries away—use them up. The Internet is a great resource for this kind of neo-retro-homemaking advice. Here's a blog post I wrote on this subject—including a recipe for homemade pizza dough that can serve as the dinner vehicle for all kinds of spare ingredients floating around in your crisper drawer:

> I am in love with my family's membership in a CSA farm this summer. But you know, those greens, they are a challenge sometimes—the tops of all those beets, turnips, kohlrabi. Yikes. What to do with all those greens?
>
> I like to throw them into quiches and vegetable tarts, into soups, and sautéed into pasta dishes. But my friend Connie had a great idea too: sauté them and put them on pizza. Yes! Oh, but don't give in to temptation and pick up an expensive pre-made pizza shell from the grocery. Make your own homemade pizza dough. It's economical, it's delicious, and it's oh so easy. (Obviously, you could also add any other pizza

toppings you'd like: onions and olives would be especially good.)

Easy Homemade Pizza Dough: *Start with 1 cup flour (white, whole-wheat, or half and half; I always use all whole-wheat). Put in a large bowl and add 1/2 tsp. salt, 1 packet of Quick Yeast (any brand, but make sure it's the quick-rising kind), 1 T. olive oil, and any seasonings you might like (half a teaspoon or so each of oregano, basil, garlic powder, or nothing at all).*

Mix the above and then add 1 cup warm water (from the tap is fine). Then add enough WHITE flour-gradually-to make a nice dough. You'll know it when you see it. I add by 1/3 cup at a time, and usually add a total of a cup, I think. Turn dough onto a floured surface and knead until it's a nice smooth ball.

Shape onto a greased pizza pan. Top with sauce, any toppings you like (greens! greens!), and cheese. Bake at 400 degrees for 15-20 minutes.

This has become one of my family's all-time favorite dinners, by the way—not bad for an economical entrée borne out of the need to use up beet greens and the conviction that take-out pizza is way too expensive.

Scale back birthday parties.

Listen, three-year-olds do not need a rented-out swimming pool or a giant bounce house. No one needs a fifty-dollar bakery cake. If you think the amount of money you spend on extravagant venues, games, decorations, and favors is what makes children happy, you couldn't be more wrong. Kids want the people who love them around them, a cake with candles, birthday presents, and a few games. Throw in some balloons and you're good. Truly.

Seek out unconventional, less expensive places to shop.

Where I live, one local gas station chain offers the cheapest milk, butter, eggs, bananas, and bread in town—by far. Guess where I buy all my milk, butter, eggs, bananas, and bread? It may seem odd, but I do buy my staples at the gas station.

Go with hand-me-downs and secondhand clothes and toys, particularly when your kids are young enough to not know or care.

This is a major way to save money. Later on, when children get older, they typically aren't amenable to used toys or their cousins' old clothes; so use these years, when they don't know anything else and will never care, to get away with spending little to no cash on their wardrobes and toy chests. Okay, so it's not all super-hip or the latest and greatest. Get over it. Your kids are.

When and if you do buy new school clothes for your children, do so the week after school starts, when all the new fall clothes go on sale.

I don't know about where you live, but in Minnesota the weather during the first few weeks of school is not noticeably different than it is in August. Send them to school in shorts and tees, and buy the cords and long-sleeved shirts during week two or three, at considerable savings.

Eat meatless meals more often.

Meat is expensive, and not even all that healthy. Switch to vegetarian entrees a few times a week, using beans and legumes for protein rather than meat, poultry, or fish, and you'll slash your grocery bill by a surprising amount.

Shamelessly ask grandparents for help.

If they have the means, most grandparents love to dote on their grandchildren. They may not know how tight your budget currently is, but would be happy to help out with preschool tuition or money for groceries if only you asked.

Take advantage of every single free event available.

When you start really paying attention, you discover that most cities offer a multitude of free events each week, month, or season. Outdoor concerts, farmers' markets, school plays, choir concerts, art exhibits, summer festivals, story hours, outdoor ice-skating, building tours, amateur sports matches, guided nature walks, and fun runs/walks abound. Each free recreational event is another day of fun for your kids that doesn't cost you a thing.

One last caveat about all these money-saving strategies: don't try to—or feel you need to—give up every single small pleasure in your life. This is simply too depressing. If you eliminate every little treat in your daily existence in an effort to save every penny you'll end up demoralized. And what kind of family life is that? Keep a few things going on that cost money, and aren't strictly necessary, but make your life worth living. (For me, those things include hanging baskets of outdoor flowers to spruce up my yard each summer, salon highlights, and a subscription to *The New Yorker*. Try to take those things from me and I will fight you.)

Positive Benefits of All This Penny-Pinching

Doesn't giving up and cutting down and living frugally make you feel all noble and smug and responsible? No? Well, kind of? But the rest of the time it can get kind of tedious and difficult? Take heart. Not only will these strategies become second nature to you if you keep them up, and eventually not feel all that hard at all anymore, but they deliver some major positive benefits as well. Besides helping your bank account, I mean.

You can rock the stay-at-home mom job longer.

Isn't this what you're doing it all for? The less money you need to live, the less your household needs you to return to work ASAP. Consider all these belt-tightening steps as staying-at-home insurance. Spend less, stay home with your kiddos for a longer part of their childhoods—maybe even the entire thing.

You'll be teaching your children better values.

Do you really want your kids to grow up thinking that money is everything, that one's material possessions are the measure of one's worth, that money equals happiness and love, that things are more important than people, fulfillment, and joy? Of course not. Live a more frugal life, and you send a very important message to your children, one that is scarce in modern society: that you can live a rich life without being rich, and that the intangibles of love, joy, and peace are what make life worth living—not the latest video game or a three-car garage.

You'll be helping the environment.

Overconsumption, overproduction, and a culture of disposable goods equal more junk in our landfills, more pollution from manufacturing and shipping goods, and a larger carbon footprint. The less you buy, the better for the earth. Period.

You're giving your children more experiences rather than more things.

Experiences are what provide long-lasting happiness and good memories, not material possessions. It makes sense, doesn't it? Aren't you more likely to remember with love and joy that afternoon you went sledding with your parents over Christmas vacation than the brand and price of the snow gear they bought you to wear while doing it?

A small house = a closer family.

A preschool teacher I once knew, whose family never moved out of their first, modest starter house even when her husband became dean of the local private college and they surely could have afforded to, said this to me once. She insisted that the trend toward new, cavernous houses with multiple floors, many bedrooms, and a bathroom for each family member actually discouraged family closeness and warmth, as each member of the family retreated to his or her own space during free time rather than gathering in more modest, common rooms to share one another's company. Take that, big mansion on the hill!

Your family will eat more healthfully.

As soon as you cut down on (or cut out) restaurant eating, packaged foods, processed snacks, convenience foods, pizza take-out, fast food, soda, juices, and sports drinks, your family's empty-calorie tally gets slashed along with your food expenses. Home cooking and whole, natural food is not only cheaper but much, much healthier than the alternatives. Now that's something you can really feel good about.

Your kids will probably be more physically active.

When you don't have as much money for toys and costly structured activities or events, your kids tend to engage in more outdoor play. Running around the backyard, climbing trees, playing kickball, tossing a football, and playing tag and hide-and-seek and hopscotch are all free—and healthy for growing bodies.

Consider Your Money-Making Options

If all this money-saving advice is well and good, but you're still desperate for a little extra cash to make ends meet (or simply to afford some "treats" from time to time, whether that be, for you, a soy latte or an expensive haircut), sit down and seriously consider all your options.

Some common money-making strategies for stay-at-home moms include part-time work (evenings and/or weekends if you don't want to or can't afford childcare during work hours), a work-from-home job, even starting your own small home-based business. Some moms are able to charge for their skills and expertise—alterations, freelance writing, tutoring, teaching a home-school class, party-planning, medical transcription, translation, graphic design, interior design, photography,—the list goes on and on—and take on work as independent contractors/consultants. Others have a talent for creating original items that people want to buy, and can earn extra income by sewing, crafting, designing and making cards, making candles or soaps, refurnishing secondhand furniture, growing food for farmers' markets, doing calligraphy, making homemade jams and preserves, or baking.

Another potential money-making strategy is to provide a service for customers who don't have the time, interest, or ability to do particular tasks themselves and are willing to outsource them for a fee. Some ideas are: dog-walking, doing laundry, preparing homemade meals, grocery shopping, packing and delivering kids' school lunches, and housecleaning.

If you're willing and able to open up your home to others, you may consider becoming a home daycare provider or renting out a spare room. And, of course, if you're the outgoing and social type, there are plenty of home-based direct sales companies with which you can sign on to be a consultant: Avon, Tupperware, Mary Kay, Arbonne, and various food, cookware and jewelry companies.

Some creative-thinking moms track down ways to work for things other than, but just as valuable as, cash. Consider the mom who provides clerical work for a small private kindergarten in exchange for reduced tuition, the mom who trades child-care services at the gym for a free membership, the mom who waters a store's parking-lot flowerbeds in exchange for a steep retail discount. There are more ways than you might think to get your financial needs met!

Be creative, keep an open mind, and think hard about what skills and interests you have that could supplement your family's income, or provide some valuable benefits you otherwise could not afford.

The Take-Home Message

Whether living a one-income life in a two-income world is a major stretch for your family or something you don't need to worry much about, the bottom line (so to speak) is the same. You are making a noble, informed choice about how you want your children raised and what you want their childhood to look like, and you should be proud of that choice. If money is tight, at times you may feel more nervous than noble, and like your free will has been hijacked by your mortgage interest rate or the rising cost of groceries, but make no mistake: you're giving a gift to your children by being home with them, and you made that decision for a reason.

You'll never regret the time you spent at home with your babies. Money, jobs, income, and bills come and go, but fifty years from now, I guarantee, you will *not* be looking back and wishing you had more material possessions. You will not be saying, *Boy, I really wish I'd spent less time with my children and more time earning money.* I promise you that.

NINE

NOTES TO MY ROOKIE
STAY-AT-HOME SELF

REMEMBER BACK in Chapter 1, when we talked about adjustment to stay-at-home motherhood, with all its modern-day busyness and unique ability to make you feel like a total rookie at everything important? Yes, well, the nice thing is, over your weeks and months and (maybe) years of being a stay-at-home mom, you change and learn and get better at all this. And I'm not just talking about your increased skill at surreptitiously ripping open a mini-Snickers bar without your preschooler in the other room hearing the crinkle of the wrapper. Although that skill can be useful.

Every stay-at-home mom moves from her own version of rookie to her own version of pro during her time at home raising children. We learn a lot of lessons and develop our own ingenious strategies for making daily life with small children work most of the time, and it means that what used to feel confusing and overwhelming is now the "new normal"; it's now a total non-issue, the notion of taking three children to the grocery store at one time.

And it also means that there are bigger lessons we have learned, beyond the shortcuts for cooking dinner and the best way to keep a baby occupied while you're on an important phone call. The more fundamental lessons are the things we wish we could go back and tell our rookie at-home mom selves, the things we wish we'd known back when motherhood, and stay-at-home motherhood, was new—things that would've made life a lot easier in those early days, or if not easier, at least easier to accept.

Those fundamental principles of the job that don't fit neatly into any specific section of this book are gathered here. Some won't ring true for you. Don't feel you have to accept unquestioned every piece of advice and knowledge thrown your way. On the other hand, stay open-minded and maybe in hindsight you will see how being open to a potential truism will free you in some unexpected way, in some unexpected moment.

Practical Magic

Here are a few of the more practical, yet still fundamental, principles I've learned as an experienced stay-at-home mom, grouped into the categories of Sleep, Supplies, Naptime, Stages, and Schedule.

Sleep ...

You can survive on way less sleep than you ever thought possible.

Remember back in college, when you thought you were really, really busy, but in reality you somehow had time to take naps? How did that work, exactly? I'll tell you how: *you weren't that busy.* Or, rather, you were what you used to think of as busy, and what a lot of people besides you thought of as busy, until you had a baby and realized that the busy-but-nap-including life of a college student is to new motherhood as, uh....taking a nap is to getting up every two hours to nurse a baby overnight.

Before having a baby, I believed I needed (needed!) 9-1/2 hours of sleep per night to be at my best. Eight hours was adequate, but anything less and I was veering into suboptimal functioning territory. Then I became a mother and learned, as have millions of parents before me, that sleep is to some degree an optional luxury. Sure, you may be bleary, cranky, fuzzy-minded, and somewhat miserable during the weeks—and dare I say months and, for some of us unlucky souls, *years?*—of night-wakings, but it will not kill you. Truly. And once you know that, it's a huge relief. You'll get through. Everyone does.

That reminds me:

An easy sleeper is pretty much pure luck.

Now *there's* something I wish someone who knew better than I did would have told me back when I was struggling with an infant who didn't nap more than 20 minutes at a time for ten straight weeks—a newborn, no less!—and was blaming myself for somehow, some way, getting it wrong day after day after day. What "it" was, I didn't know exactly, but I did know that no one else's baby wouldn't nap at four months old. So what was I doing wrong?

If I could go back in time, I'd tell that younger, new-mom me that the answer was: "Nothing." That it was simply my unfortunate luck to get a poor sleeper. That there is evidence showing that babies born from long, complicated, and stressful labors (oh boy, mine to a T!) exhibit neurological characteristics that manifest in fussy temperaments, poor sleep behaviors, and an inability to self-soothe. And that there are always those babies who had uncomplicated births but are just tough nuts when it comes to sleep habits. That my friends with "good-sleeper" babies were lucky.

I didn't know it then, but I'm telling it to any of you now who are in my former, exhausted, self-berating, confused shoes.

Relatedly, you cannot force a child to sleep.

After seven years and two children, lesson learned! Best to accept this one from the start. Yes, you can implement good sleep habits. You can establish naptime and bedtime routines. You can "sleep-train." You can stick to a sleep schedule, buy room-darkening blinds for the nursery, and read every sleep book out there. In fact, many of those things are helpful. However, when it comes right down to it, there's nothing you can do to guarantee your child will lie down, close her eyes, shut her mouth, and go to sleep. Want proof of me learning this the hard way? Here is a blog post from a few Christmases ago:

> *The very, very painful lesson I have learned this week is that Genevieve will no longer take two naps a day. If, in response to her eye-rubbing and fussing, you put her down for the old familiar morning nap–even if you wake her up in 45-60 minutes so she won't nap too long–she will NOT take her afternoon nap. Will. Not.*
>
> *Then she will be so tired by 6 p.m. (at which point she has not slept in eight hours) that, when you try to nurse her for bedtime, she will fall heavily asleep within five minutes, sucking lazily in her sleep in a decidedly non-drinking manner.*
>
> *However. If you keep her up in the morning, because you realize she is an old baby now who is giving up her morning nap, do not go around thinking she will then*

sleep for a good two or three hours in the afternoon. Because you will be wrong, and when she wakes up in 45-60 minutes, and it's not even 2 p.m., you will be sorely disappointed. Or maybe LOSING YOUR EVER-LOVING MIND is a better way to describe what you will be.

So I guess that's two lessons I learned this week. I hope Santa is good to me this year.

Save yourself a whole lot of frustration and learn this lesson far earlier than I did. Cannot. Force a child to sleep. Terribly frustrating. But true.

Supplies . . .

Outfit each level of your house with a changing station.

Because you will not want to be running upstairs every time your baby needs a diaper change. It doesn't have to be elaborate. Save the changing table furniture for the nursery; just plant a big basket in a handy nook somewhere—under the coffee table, or in a corner of the living room—and stock it with diapers, wipes, diaper rash cream, and baby powder, along with receiving blankets to use as changing pads when changing diapers on the floor or sofa. A few extra outfits might be wise too, including socks.

Keep a lot of stuff in your car.

No, no, I don't mean empty Starbucks cups in the cup holders and crushed animal crackers in the crevices of your toddler's car seat. But I do mean almost everything else: extra diapers, wipes, plastic bags, a plastic bin of board books within child-arms' reach, full kiddo outfits (including socks), Kleenex, lip balm, hand sanitizer, a lidded plastic container of dry Cheerios. Believe me, a stash of essentials in the place where you spend the most time other than your home is crucial. And while the above items are probably pretty obvious, there are a few others that might not be so obvious, but that can salvage an entire afternoon.

Consider a sturdy canvas tote bag filled with sand toys, for bringing out at the playground when interest in climbing equipment wanes, but digging and play-cooking in the pea-gravel or playground mulch might buy you an extra half hour of gabbing on a park bench with your mama friends. Consider an extra-light stroller, folded up and stowed in the trunk, for those times you didn't plan on walking around but now would like to walk around. Consider a picnic blanket, for spreading out on the grass at the park for the non-mobile baby to sit on with his baby toys, or for impromptu al fresco snacks. Consider, once your babes are out of diapers, a spare potty chair. Yes. You heard me. A potty chair in the back of your vehicle. Believe me, either you'll never use this, or one day you'll want to fall to your knees in thanks that you actually have such a thing in your car. Very likely the latter.

Naptime & Schedule . . .

Cook dinner during naptime.

This may be my all-time favorite and most successful go-to strategy for at-home mothering. You would be amazed at how many dishes you can make in advance with no ill effects. (And you know what? In the early days, you won't even care about ill effects. Is dinner made? Then you're good.)

This tip may not be so integral when your baby is very young; but as he grows, and you want your after-nap afternoon hours to be free for those all-important socializing opportunities—you know, the playdates and park meet-ups with other moms that make your late afternoons bearable. You will love having the cooking done beforehand, so you can stay out longer and not worry about dinner prep. (Or come home early and still not worry about dinner prep!) I have been known to prepare just about anything hours before dinner, including pasta, baked chicken, burritos, casseroles, meatloaf, roasted vegetables, even rice. And of course things like chili, soups, and stews get better with time. There's always the slow cooker, too: throw something in during morning cartoons and let it cook all day with no help from you. Score! As for everything else, remember: anything can be reheated.

Do chores during naptime. Or, never ever do chores during naptime.

Truly, there are two schools of thought on this, which may be related to the age of one's kiddos. When your children are very young babies and toddlers, and your sleep deficit is larger than the federal budget deficit (or so it seems), you might want to adopt the latter policy. This period of stay-at-home mothering life is so physically exhausting that to use precious naptime to mop the floors may be utterly soul-crushing. You may not actually use your baby's naptime to nap yourself, but surfing the Internet, reading a magazine, drinking a cup of tea, or watching daytime television may be the recharging you need during those precious short hours of down-time when your babies are small.

But a little later on, you may find that naptime is the ideal time to zip through a few household chores, because you can get them done far faster if you don't have a three-year-old attached to your hip during your efforts. This might allow you to relax and enjoy the time after nap, when you're playing with your kids, a little bit more, since you don't also have to be brooding about not getting the dishes done or balancing the checkbook.

So maybe the lesson here is, *Use naptime in whatever way benefits you the most at the time, and then don't think twice or feel guilty about it.*

And I can honestly say that is a lesson I have learned thoroughly and well.

Utilize structure and scheduling. Except for when structure and scheduling are not possible.

Listen, I'm a big fan of the schedule. My opinion is that structure and scheduling are key in keeping the modern stay-at-home mom, who may have less company around her in the form of next-door or across-the-street fellow stay-at-home moms than her mother did before her, from going bananas at home alone all day.

What do I mean by "schedule"? Well, this time I'm not talking about when and how you clean house. I'm talking about the rhythm and rituals of your day at home with babies and children before they are old enough to attend preschool—the months and years when they are with you, all day every day.

Days at home with very small children, especially before those children are verbal—when it's often just you literally talking to yourself for eight or nine hours a day—tend to take on a life of their own. The problem is that sometimes that life resembles a coma. (Except without the restful, lying-still qualities.) Those hours at home alone with babies can get really, really boring. Not boring as in "nothing to do." But boring as in *Oh my God I can't believe I've been up since five and it's only ten a.m. and I have to get through eight more hours of baby-care alone before my spouse comes home to keep me company and give me a break.*

It took me a while to figure this out, but the way to make your at-home baby-stage days more enjoyable, productive and stimulating is to establish a daytime rhythm for yourself and the baby, inserting your own choice of activity between the required tasks of diapering, naps, meals, etc., to provide the open hours with some definition and predictability.

It doesn't have to—indeed, shouldn't—be rigid, non-negotiable, or supermom-like. It doesn't have to—and really, *really* shouldn't—include daily quizzing of your toddler with alphabet flash cards or sitting your preschooler down in front of "Teach-Your-Baby-French!" CDs. The kind of schedule I'm talking about is one that breaks up the long expanse of day into a self-styled, familiar rhythm, with chunks of identifiable tasks or activities in mind, to give you the structure and purpose humans crave.

Here's how you might break the day into "chunks":

- ✓ Wake up, breakfast, etc.
- ✓ Morning block #1: morning nap or a walk
- ✓ Morning block #2: outdoor play, library storytime, or errands (depending on the day)
- ✓ Lunch, nap
- ✓ Afternoon block #1: free play with toys
- ✓ Afternoon block #2: art project
- ✓ Dinner, bath, bed

Of course, the activities will need to be adapted for different stages. Your schedule will change when your baby is no longer taking morning naps, for example. And keep in mind that a schedule like this is not meant to be set in stone. If you find yourself anxiously checking a written daytime agenda and stressing out because you never got around to an art project, for example, you're missing the point. The idea is simply that chunking your day into small portions with a general idea of what you could do with each chunk can make your amorphous day much more manageable.

And now for the inevitable newborn-stage caveat: remember what I said about structure and scheduling not always being possible? When your baby is brand-new—anywhere from one day old to, say, four to six months old, depending on the infant— there is no such thing as a schedule, not for most of us anyway. Don't fall into the trap of thinking that you're doing something wrong because someone asked you if "the baby's on a schedule yet." When my first baby was a newborn, people did this to me all the time, plus I kept reading all these parenting magazine articles and glossy promotional booklets that came in the mail with baby food coupons, and they all urged me to "Put the baby on a schedule!" For the life of me I couldn't figure out what they meant. People kept quoting formulas like this one: "Eat, play, sleep; eat, play, sleep." And I kept thinking, *Um, she falls asleep while she's nursing; what am I supposed to do then?*

Later on, I learned that newborns rarely fall into schedules, no matter what their parents try to do. A vague, changeable rhythm may be detectable early on, but "scheduling" the baby— easing her into a consistent routine of, say, taking the morning nap 90 minutes after awakening for the day, and the afternoon nap at one, feeding and playing in predictable sessions in between—typically becomes possible at about six months old, more or less. And from then on, I'm for it, 100%.

Just realize that routine, structure, and schedules can save your life—or terrorize it. Don't even think about it at first, and then run with it later.

The Early Stages...

Relax more when the babies are young.

I don't just mean the idea we already discussed, the notion of napping or resting when the baby naps. I mean relax in a broader sense. The truth is, while the early-baby years are anything but relaxing in most ways—after all, there's the sleep deprivation and the colic and the diapers and the fact that you have to pack what seems like your entire house into your diaper bag and car when you try to go anywhere—in some ways the time when your babies are small does give you some opportunities to treat yourself that you won't often see later on.

Now that my daughters are mobile, aware, observant, cognizant children rather than unquestioning, game little babies who don't care if a nearby adult is watching *Oprah* or eating chocolate, I often wonder why I didn't do more of those things when I could. There are so many things I don't want my daughters exposed to now that I truly miss their previous lack of awareness. You can't watch *The Today Show* during breakfast when your children are beyond toddler age; all that violence on the news? Forget it! You can't listen to much pop music if you don't want to have to explain the occasional four-letter word. You can't eat popcorn for dinner if you don't want your kids to.

It's true that when I was first at home with my firstborn baby, I did sometimes watch daytime TV while I nursed her, and snacked on the Halloween candy I'd bought early for trick-or-treaters. Now and then—but not often—we went to the corner coffee-shop for a pastry breakfast. There were occasional days when I read *People* magazine while the baby bounced in her jumper. But mostly I overachieved—or tried to. I spent a lot of time worrying if incidental exposure to *Oprah* was damaging to a baby's brain. I worried that tummy time wasn't long enough, and that sometimes I skipped it. I kept busy. I had an agenda, and if I didn't get it all accomplished I felt fairly bad about it. After all, I was home all day! Shouldn't I be weeding the garden and washing the windows rather than, I don't know, sitting on the patio with an iced coffee while the baby naps or plays nearby?

Then there's the way you lose your unstructured freedom once your children reach a certain age. You can't spend half the morning baking cupcakes in your pj's when you've got to get children to preschool on time, and eventually late afternoons have to include homework more often than *Oprah*. There are many wonderful things about having bigger kids. But you miss the days when you could make your own schedule and inject some adult luxuries into your day without having to explain yourself to a curious preschooler. Of course one day those children will all be old enough to go to school all day long, and then you can relax while they're off in first grade. But most likely by then you'll have other things to do.

My advice is to relax more when your children are little. Give yourself permission to be nice to yourself when no one's going to give you a hard time about whipped cream in your coffee or not getting dressed right away in the morning. The baby doesn't care; why should you? You're working really, really hard when you're a stay-at-home mom to an infant. Baby yourself too, whenever you can, because while it's always appropriate to treat yourself well, there are some ways of relaxing that, once the baby years are over, you probably won't experience again for some time.

For that matter, get away with whatever you can while your children are little.

This applies to any number of situations: dressing them in hand-me-downs or garage-sale-find kid clothes, trolling the used baby-gear stores for secondhand toys for birthdays and Christmas, keeping birthday parties simple and small (or even skipping them altogether in favor of cupcakes around the dinner table on birthday night), making trick-or-treating on Halloween consist of knocking on the five doors on your block and nothing else, eschewing excessive kid exposure to media, pretending applesauce is a real dessert. The list goes on and on.

Think for a moment about the freedom that gives you.

Mamas, unless you have unlimited disposable income and good reasons for taking the time-, money-, energy-consuming route (your own personal sincere happiness, a lot of time to kill, a local grandma who wants to take on the bulk of the work or expense), take advantage of the sweet, innocent, wondrous cluelessness of the very young, and keep it small, whatever "it" may happen to be. Most likely, your bank account, energy reserves, mental health, and anyone closely related to you will thank you later on. Who needs all the crazy? Keep it simple and sweet while you can.

The Big Stuff

Here are some of the weightier lessons I've learned over the past several years as a stay-at-home mom. Because while making dinner in advance is good, wouldn't you like to know what you should tell yourself the next time you're on the verge of a mothering nervous breakdown?

You don't have to be perfect.

Seriously. I know you know this one intellectually, but most of us dedicated moms drive a hard bargain with ourselves. Who among us hasn't lain awake at night worrying that we're not doing a good enough job as moms? I know that when I became a mom, I was surprised that being a good parent felt harder to achieve than graduating Phi Beta Kappa or becoming board-certified as a doctoral-degreed clinical psychologist.

It's hard not to think you need to be the perfect mom: never raising your voice, quick with crafty art project ideas, cooking organic food from scratch each day, consistently coming up with just the right disciplinary tactic for every possible situation, always saying the right thing (which might *not* be: "Good Lord in heaven, you are going to turn all my hair gray!"). But the sooner you recognize the truth that there's no such thing as a perfect mom, the sooner you can pat yourself on the back for your efforts, and forgive yourself your mistakes. Maybe when you make a really big mistake, like I did back when my first daughter was two and my second was just six weeks old, instead of flogging yourself for it, you'll just sigh and blog about it:

Well, I survived my first day alone as a stay-at-home mom to two babies! You could say that I was a bit scattered today as I juggled all the goings-on and the incessant baby needs. For example—and I am loath to admit this—when we got home from playgroup I discovered that Genevieve had ridden the entire way home WITH HER CAR SEAT STRAPS UNBUCKLED.

And our playdate was a good twenty minutes away on rural county highways, too—we're not talking about a two-block jaunt or something like that. Good Lord, I just about fainted when I saw it.

Here's what happened. At playgroup, Genevieve fell asleep in my arms and I set her in her car seat to nap, unbuckled of course, with a baby blanket completely over her torso and up to her chin. In the hubbub of leaving group, what with four toddlers and three newborns testing the patience of four moms, and hungry tummies beginning to growl, I picked up the car seat as-is, without a second thought, and clicked it into the car to drive home before my entourage's tenuous hold on good humor evaporated. Never even noticed, never even remembered, that Genevieve was just loose in her seat, snoozing away under her snuggly blanket.

Everyone survived, of course. But talk about a dicey way to be reminded that it's not only the newbie mom who makes the rookie mistakes.

Oh, and then there are the mistakes that are more about making unfortunate choices in the heat of the moment than they are about innocent gaffes. I once overheard my daughter out me to my visiting mother-in-law by saying, in reference to an old board book that at one time had a doll attached to the cover, "That book used to have a ballerina on the front, but it broke off when Mama got really mad one time and threw the book on the floor." I was standing on the stairway landing at the time where they couldn't see me, and I actually winced and crept back upstairs. I noticed as I crept that there was only solemn silence from my mother-in-law in response. But then I rolled my eyes, because, seriously, is anyone outing me for the times I do selfless, good-mama things like sleep on the floor in the hallway outside the nursery for days on end when my toddler wouldn't stop crying at bedtime? No, they are not.

We all do noble, admirable parenting things at times—lots of times!—but no matter how old your children, how many you have, or how long you've been doing this parenting thing, you will always fall prey to the blunders, dust-ups, and freak-outs that make us all human. We all do. It's okay to be imperfect. In fact, there's no other way to be.

It's okay to love at-home motherhood and hate at-home motherhood simultaneously.

Now *there's* an important lesson learned! Isn't that a strange idea, though? That you can both love and hate something, especially something so noble, so *important*, as mothering? But it's true, and it's normal, and that's an absolutely crucial message to give yourself from your very first day on the stay-at-home mom job. For all the discussion of motherhood in the media these days—the glamorizing of celebrity moms, the debates over the "mommy wars," the witty first-person essays in parenting magazines—we still don't talk truly openly about the times we hate it, and how guilty that makes us feel. But there's nothing more comforting than knowing you're not alone in your feelings and experiences.

No one wanted to be a mother more than I did, I believed wholeheartedly. After a year and a half of infertility struggles, I cherished my first pregnancy and the impending birth of my baby with every cell in my body. Even the nausea and heartburn and aching hip ligaments were fine with me; they all meant I was on my way to living my dream of having a family, of raising babies. So I felt like the worst person in the world when I came home from the hospital after 60 sleepless hours of back labor and a physically traumatic delivery and, when my newborn daughter cried and I knew I had no choice but to nurse her no matter how sore and exhausted and overwhelmed I felt, I sobbed and said, "I don't like this job!"

And that was only day one! Thankfully, that was probably the hardest day of the job. I'm pretty sure everything gets easier after you've survived 60 hours of back labor.

Think of stay-at-home motherhood as, sometimes and in some ways, a job just like any other job: one with parts you love with the heat of a thousand suns, and parts that leave you counting the minutes till quitting time, which, of course, never comes. Once you give yourself permission to consider your current day, night, and everything-in-between job as similar in some ways to that other job you left to do this one, you'll feel better about realizing that everyone who loves their job also hates certain aspects of it. And that includes great moms like you.

Don't be afraid to live your values, no matter what the other moms do or say.

For some reason, moms sometimes become judgmental and evangelistic about their parenting and life choices—competitive, even. In raising a family (as in everything else in life, too, by the way), you've either got to trust your instincts, your passions, your world-view and life philosophy, and be confident in your parenting decisions, or else resort to doubting yourself, questioning your parenting abilities when compared to those of others you know, and potentially resorting to criticism or snarkiness when confronted with any idea that doesn't resemble your own. Believe me, the latter is a tough road.

Parenting and family values are hard to navigate. Yours may not match your mom's, your sister's, your neighbor's, or even your best friend's. The key to inner peace in this area is recognizing this truism early in your parenting journey. There will always be other moms who do things very differently from you. That doesn't mean their way is the right way for you.

If you consistently and confidently live your own parenting values, you will always be right for your own particular circumstance and your own family. Did you get that? You are right about what to do *for your own family*. You're the expert. You're right. Repeat: You. Are. Right.

And, finally, for all of our rookie selves, the most fundamental lesson of parenting is one Mom probably recited to you many times, as you suffered acne or failed romance or the hardest college class ever:

This, too, shall pass.

I know you know it. Sometimes, of course, the notion of everything passing can be melancholy and nostalgic. But this sage reminder is more for those times of mothering strife when you seriously wonder if you can go on—what with the crying at bedtime and the tantrums, or the colic and the fussy, shapeless afternoons that last a century apiece. It will pass, all of it. The good, yes, but the very, very bad too. And if there's one thing you learn as an experienced mom, it's that sometimes that one simple little reminder can reframe your entire day. The super, super hard parts? They, too—as everything!—will pass. Just don't think too much about how that also applies to the parts you like, and you'll be fine.

TEN

THE YEARS ARE SHORT:

MINDFUL PARENTING

WHEN MY DAUGHTERS were toddlers and life was at its most chaotic and exhausting, an experienced mom friend with children ten years older than mine, who remembered well the long, challenging days of at-home motherhood, said to me, "You know what they say: the days are long, but the years are short."

Well, I don't know who "they" are, but boy are they right. No matter how much you love being home with your children, there are days—many of them, in fact—that seem to stretch on into infinity, when you feel that you'll forever be stuck there by the patio door, listening to your two-year-old scream simultaneously about wanting to put her shoes on by herself and about the fact that she *cannot get her shoes on by herself.* You cannot take it. The day must be 100 hours long. No, wait. This tantrum, alone, seems 100 hours long.

But then, in the mere blink of an eye, that toddler has a backpack on her shoulders and she's climbing onto the school bus for her first day of kindergarten. At which point, if you're like me, you are absolutely stunned—I mean, seriously: where did the years go?!—and also beset with tears, although you hold those tears until after the bus pulls away so that she can't see your courage wavering.

This is what I wrote about the slow-fast passage of time, when my older daughter was finishing up preschool:

My firstborn daughter's fifth birthday is six weeks away, and I've recently begun to consider some birthday party plans. Five years! How can it be? Is that even possible? I sit here and think about how big she is, how long five years really is, and truth be told, I can hardly remember the actual details of her infant self, of how she felt on my shoulder or how she looked in her crib. You think you'll never forget these things, but you do.

A lot happens in five years! You go from total neophyte parent, completely ignorant of all things baby, steeped in the kind of naïve idiocy you can hardly fathom now— How could we have been confused by the introduction of solid food? Why did it seem so complicated? Or, Can you believe we didn't know we'd never really sleep again?—all the way to experienced mother of two, with the rhythms of baby/toddler-parenting so ingrained in your existence that when a childless friend asks you, "How does a person know she's ready to give up all her selfish needs, her freedom, and have a baby?", you actually give some surely incomprehensible response about it not being that hard, really, about how when it's your own baby you just do it and it's fine in the end.

It's as if you don't even remember the years of sleep deprivation and fatigue-induced panic, the hours of colic-crying, the months of nursing every two hours around the clock and a baby who wouldn't take a bottle, the times you went for weeks without speaking to another adult during the day, just paced back and forth across the floor with a fussy infant, wondering what you were doing wrong and how you'd ever survive it. You look at your nearly-five-year-old daughter now and you think, well, here we are, and look at this big kid I've got here, with her jokes and large vocabulary and ability to brush her own teeth. You don't think about how when you first brought her home from the hospital she cried every single night from 7 p.m. to 4 a.m. for the first four weeks of her life.

Except when you do. And then five years seems so, so short-just a flash, really.

The other day I was talking to a friend of mine with kids my girls' ages, and we were bemoaning the usual minor conundrums of preschooler-parenting life-what to bring for school snack, the healthy option or the cheap one-and I said to her, "Just think though: in ten years the things we'll be concerned about will be missed curfews and dating and keeping them from alcohol and drugs and having sex too soon, and we'll look back on the question of preschool snack as the ultimate luxury when it comes to parenting worries. 'Oh, if only our biggest concern was how healthy their preschool snack is!' we'll say to each other! 'Remember when our biggest worry was preschool snack?!'"

So there you have it. Five years is really short. And also really long. And then short again. And sometimes long.

And I have a feeling that's how it's going to go for the rest of life.

It's important to remind yourself, on those days when the minutes seem like hours, that the years really are short. That doesn't mean you're wrong to bemoan those long, long days. Who wouldn't? But it might make them a little easier to withstand if you remember just how brief your children's childhoods really are.

Practicing Mindfulness

There are moments of parenting that you understandably wish away. Listening to a two-year-old's tantrum comes to mind. But have you ever noticed that we seem to "wish away" all kinds of moments, in the form of multitasking, checking our watches or cells or e-mail every few minutes, constantly thinking about the next thing we have to do, right after this sweet or mundane or amazing or calm or interesting or challenging or fun moment with our kids?

If you've ever heard, or read, or studied anything about Buddhism, you're probably familiar with the notion of living each moment as fully as possible, existing within it rather than fighting against it, observing rather than resisting, appreciating instead of anticipating whatever's coming next. Oh, how the notion of living in the moment could benefit our mothering lives! How much calmer and more relaxed we would be if, instead of obsessively watching the clock, willing the tedious or challenging minutes away, we adopted the Zen-like attitude of: "It is what it is."

A friend of mine describes this attitude as "doing to be doing, not doing to be done," and says she adopts it when shoveling snow in the middle of a typical days-long Minnesota snowfall, when, even as you're shoveling, your work is getting erased by the next wave of precipitation. But I think it applies just as well to parenting small children (come to think of it, especially parenting young children during a days-long Minnesota snowfall).

Stay-at-home mothering isn't about getting to the finish line of the craft project, the board game, the meal, the morning, the day, the shoe-tying lesson, the preschool years. It's really about the actual doing of these things, the shepherding and teaching and experiencing and enjoying of the little beings you helped create. And training yourself to live each moment of those processes is the essence of mindful parenting.

No one gets a prize when the dried pasta has been successfully glued onto the cardboard. There's no promotion for getting two toddlers fully bundled into snow clothes. (Maybe there should be!) It's about the doing, not about the being done—because, let's face it, parenting is never done.

The next time you experience impatience with the daily challenges of mothering, try practicing a mindful approach to whatever's going on. Take a deep breath and remind yourself that each moment passes, the good and the bad, and your job is simply to be there and live it.

One reason this Zen-like attitude is essential is that, with growing children, you will almost never know that the last time of anything—nursing, falling asleep while sucking on a blankie, pronouncing "yogurt" as "doga"—is in fact the last. Therefore, while it is impossible to maintain perfect mindfulness at all times when parenting small children all day—indeed, most of the time your version of "mindfulness" may involve being painfully aware of how much you'd pay at any given moment for more sleep than you are presently getting—it's worth it to try. Slow down and appreciate the slippery rushes of child development as they happen.

When I knew my second baby was going to be my last, it really hit home to me just how final each passing stage of baby-parenting was:

The thing about thinking that you're probably not going to have any more babies is that everything—every single little thing—is the last. The mourning starts right away. You're only four weeks into new-babydom, and poof!—the last mitten-sized newborn diaper you will ever use again. A week later, and goodbye tiny knitted bonnet with the ribbon ties. Another month or so? Never again the swaddling, never again the bassinet. It goes on and on; it never ends, right? Although I guess there's a bright side to the endless never-agains of parenting: I mean, surely the last night-nursing, the last potty-training accident, the last orthodontia bill, the last driving lesson—these will be causes for celebration.

And I try really hard to appreciate the present moment with my baby, because the thing about these lasts is that you rarely, if ever, know in advance when they are coming. You just look around one day and go, Wow, when did she stop with that crazy full-belly, split-second, phantom grin thing she used to do in her sleep? Or, When did she get too big for the Pooh hat with the ears? The other day Genevieve fell asleep nursing, and though I know there will be many more instances of that occurrence in future months, I couldn't help but marvel at her heavy lids and her bear-cub snores, because one day this baby will never nurse to sleep again, but will instead twist her curious head and kick her big-baby legs and groan and giggle her way through her milky snacks, and this warm little pup crooked in just one arm will be a distant memory.

The "lasts" keep coming, and though you can't let yourself get bogged down in mourning them too much, you can occasionally stop, pause, drink in whatever sweet baby or toddler or second-grade thing your kid is doing these days, and remind yourself to memorize the moment forever. You probably won't remember it forever, of course—most things you don't, even when you think that you will—but when you practice mindfulness and appreciation just a tiny bit more, you free your mind and heart to move on to the next bit of mothering territory with joy, without regret.

Practicing Gratitude

Several years back, "gratitude" was a self-help buzzword, and counting your blessings, no matter what else was happening in your life, was all the rage. You were supposed to keep a "gratitude journal," and write in it nightly, recording which things you were grateful for that day, and then reread your notations on a regular basis. Someone even (presumably) made a healthy chunk of money by designing, publishing, and marketing a pre-formatted Gratitude Journal for women. I know because I saw it everywhere—in bookstores and gift shops and on the bookshelves and kitchen counters of my female friends.

I never kept a gratitude journal, or bought the one available at Barnes and Noble. Seeing as how I didn't have kids yet at the time, I suspect that back then my list of "gratitudes" would have centered around such indulgences as "sleeping late on weekends" and "Friday night movies" and "the occasional Dairy Queen

Blizzard dinner." I mean, sure, a good job, good health, solid marriage, and intact family would be there too. But let's not underestimate the pleasure of a Dairy Queen Blizzard for dinner.

Now that I'm a parent, gratitude has become both harder and much, much easier to come by. What I mean is that the simple pleasures of childfree life, those pockets of freedom within every childless adult's typical day, largely vanished the moment I latched my first newborn to my breast in the Methodist Hospital delivery room. I still possessed the profound, larger blessings that really count: family, health, shelter, love, food, safety, political and religious freedom, enough money to pay the bills. But I lost a lot of selfish pleasures, and I didn't feel grateful, upon entering motherhood, for the sleep deprivation, endless laundry, and soiled diapers.

At the same time, of course, my gratitude soared: A baby! A family! A child to raise, and adore, and care for, and treasure. And that gratitude only multiplied with baby number two. Parenthood is great for gratitude: you can experience a major disappointment or a stressful day or a crisis or even just a nondescript low mood, and your children still hug and kiss you, giggle, look adorable as they sleep, worship the very ground you walk on (until they're pre-teens, that is). They're still there to remind you that life is good. They'll always be your biggest, most precious accomplishment, and for that you can feel grateful every day.

But do you? On a typical day as a busy stay-at-home mom, I spend an awful lot more time managing activities, completing household tasks, rushing from one errand to the other, cooking and serving food, breaking up sibling arguments, and picking up toys than I do musing on what I'm grateful for. This is worth changing; because when you stop to remind yourself of what you're grateful for as a mom, you automatically slow down to appreciate the moment. By definition, you're practicing mindful parenting, because you're not simply focused on getting through the whiny morning or naptime rebellion or third diaper blowout of the day—you're realizing that though the days are long, the years are short.

You don't need to create a gratitude journal, although that might be nice. I encourage you, however, to begin practicing gratitude as you run the carpool or tie yet another shoe or sit down on the floor to *play Legos yet again dear God so sick of Legos the Legos may kill me*. Whenever you think of it—or whenever you feel your blood pressure beginning to spike—take a moment and say to yourself, "Today I am grateful for _____." It might not be the Legos, but that's okay. It doesn't matter what it is. Resist the urge to blow off steam by posting to Facebook or texting your best friend (you can always do that later), and instead, tell yourself what you are grateful for. Hey, tell your kids, too! Write it down if you want, or just let it sit in your brain for a minute.

There! You've just lived in the moment. You've been a mindful parent. Doesn't it feel good? Repeat often, and you'll notice yourself appreciating your life as a mom even more, feeling more blessed, and maybe even feeling less anxious or irritable on those tough days with the kiddos. Gratitude is good for one's mental health, after all. It might not slow down the years, but it might curtail a meltdown or two—yours, I mean.

BONUS CHAPTER

"SO, WHAT DO YOU DO ALL DAY?"

(SIMPLE AT-HOME KID ACTIVITIES THAT WON'T BREAK THE BANK OR DRIVE YOU CRAZY)

ONE OF THE HARDEST THINGS about being home full-time with young children is keeping them occupied for ten to twelve hours a day. Sure, when they're newborns and your daily existence is a blur of feedings, diaper changes, and the several-times-per-day outfit swap and related laundry requirements ("Oops, more spit-up!" ... "Another diaper blowout—seriously?"), you're likely to find entire mornings consumed by the seeming Herculean tasks of merely keeping everyone dressed, fed, and happy, let alone trying to get out the door for a stroller walk or a pediatrician visit. But believe me, once they're sitting up, zooming around, or speaking their minds—but before they're reading on their own or going on solo playdates—things get a whole lot more challenging when it comes to "burning daylight hours," as a mom I know once called it.

Particularly if you've been home full-time for an extended period, you don't have a part-time sitter, nanny, or preschool situation to break up your days and weeks, or you're limited in terms of transportation, budget or the weather, filling time and entertaining the kiddos (thus preserving your own sanity) can feel near impossible at times. Meals, snacks, clean-up, and naps still occupy a fair amount of the day, but as all parents know, the attention span of small children ranges from "split second" to "only long enough for me to pour myself a cup of coffee, but not actually drink it." In other words, kids don't spend much time on any one thing, and that means you need a lot of ideas in your stay-at-home mom arsenal. Otherwise, you run out of things to do at about, oh, 9:30 a.m. And then you want to bang your head against the wall for several hours on end. Believe me, I've been there. Here's one entry on *Mama in Wonderland* from a day just like that:

> *I feel like a cruise ship social director. For toddlers.*

> *Christopher's working an extra-long day today: he left before the girls were awake, and will be gone about an hour later than usual tonight. He took the car, and also it's raining. Thus, we have a long, indoor day to fill.*

> *So far today we have: made and baked homemade soft pretzels; watched part of a Wiggles DVD from the library; had a tea party for morning snack, eating homemade soft pretzels and drinking actual raspberry herbal tea in our teacups; watched the window-washers come and clean the interior and exterior of all the windows in our house; played Play-Doh; read library books; and gone "swimming" in the bathtub (with swimsuits, beach towels, etc.). And that was all before lunch.*

> *Now it is naptime, only Julia isn't napping. If anyone has any tips on filling approximately four more hours of indoor playtime, let me know. Immediately.*

Believe me, I have had plenty of days when my version of "keeping the children entertained" involved tearing out my own hair, threatening extra naps, and humming loudly while studiously ignoring the whining. But I once wrote a weekly column about keeping small children entertained, and, hey, I have several years' experience under my belt. While guidance and coaching about self-care, mindfulness, and health are all well and good, sometimes all a mama needs is a recipe for homemade finger paint.

That's why, in this bonus chapter, I've compiled a list of some simple-but-great activities for babies, toddlers, and small children. Most of them are indoor activities, though not all. Many require few if any special equipment or supplies. Most are appropriate for a span of ages, worth a shot with not just your toddling babe but also your demanding preschooler, though some are geared toward a specific developmental stage. Most importantly, the following activities aren't fancy, necessarily impressive, or complicated endeavors the likes of which you'd expect at your local private preschool, the one with the five-year waiting list. These are things you can actually do yourself, at home, with your own materials and waning energy level. I promise. Because what good would they be to the harried at-home mom otherwise?

These ideas should get you started on those days when you've got no plans for things to do beyond pouring yourself a second (or third) cup of coffee. You've probably got your own stash of at least a few ideas, and you should add those to this list—write them down and tuck them into this book, right here, to remind yourself the next time you come up blank.

I leave you here, to go on and enjoy your stay-at-home mama life. Let it be your Wonderland.

Seriously Fun Ideas For Burning Those Daylight Hours

COTTON BALL FUN

Take out a bag of cotton balls. (You have cotton balls in the house, don't you? From now on, make sure you do!) Dump them into an empty plastic bin (or large bowl, cooking pot, empty cardboard box, etc.) on the floor. Put out big plastic cooking utensils like spoons and soup ladles, as well as real or toy bowls, skillets, and measuring cups. Suggest scooping, dumping, counting, "cooking," carrying, stirring, etc.

I first "invented" this activity when my daughters were 3-1/2 years and 17 months old, and it was big hit. They did all sorts of pretend play with the cotton balls, and occupied themselves for a good 15 or 20 minutes *without me*, which is saying a lot in my house. After Julia, my then-three-year-old, tired of it, her baby sister, Genevieve, still busily toddled around the playroom depositing cotton balls here and there for quite awhile. Later, I found a bunch of them stuffed inside an empty baking-cocoa can the girls have in their play kitchen. The possibilities are endless!

Be sure to re-bag the cotton balls afterward and set them aside for future kid use. One bag of cotton balls will last a long time for things like this. (And later, you can use them for art projects.)

RICE BOX

This activity is great for toddlers (who are beyond the stage of putting everything in their mouths) and preschoolers, especially, though even kindergarten-age children can enjoy it. It's basically a sensory box, filled with materials for sifting, stirring, feeling with one's hands, scooping, and pouring. In our house, we called it a "Baby Rice Box," but you can use other contents.

To make a "Rice Box," you need a large plastic bin or box, such as the type made by Rubbermaid and used to store toys and clothes. A lid is ideal, so you can close up the box when not in use, keeping it filled and ready for when the mood next strikes. It should be large enough for a child to kneel or sit in front of it on the floor, with room to manipulate the contents inside. I used an approximately one-foot-by-three-feet rectangular clear plastic bin, though larger would be even better.

Fill the bin with a few inches of uncooked, dry rice, pasta, beans, or lentils (or a mixture). Add plastic sand toys such as small buckets, scoopers, and shovels; funnels; measuring cups or spoons; large stirring spoons; or whatever you have on hand. Set on the (preferably uncarpeted!) floor and let your child have at it! Be prepared to do a fair amount of sweeping up when he or she is done playing; it's fully worth it.

This is a great thing to have prepared and stored in an adults-only closet or cupboard, so you can take it out on those long, cold, trapped-inside winter afternoons when everyone's forgotten all about it and is excited to see it again. My girls happily played with "Genevieve's Baby Rice Box" until they were three and five years old, saving my sanity on many a midwinter late afternoon when I needed to cook dinner and occupy my daughters at the same time.

BATHTUB SOUP

Don't save baths for clean-up time only! Babies and young children love playing in the bath, and it's a real novelty to them to see you run a bath in the middle of the day, just for fun. Gather some cooking equipment you don't mind being used in the tub: think soup ladles, funnels, measuring cups and spoons, and a few small Tupperware containers. Tell your little one to make "bathtub soup." (Of course, you should never, ever leave children unattended in the tub.)

SWIMMING IN THE BATHTUB

Another fun bathtub activity, this is especially fun in the winter when the beach and swimming pool seem a million miles—and months—away. Tell your children they're going "swimming" in the bathtub, and then gather swimsuits, beach towels, and small sand shovels and buckets. Let the kids change into their swimsuits and pretend the tub is a lake, ocean, or pool. Spread towels out alongside, and encourage them to splash, blow bubbles, and pretend to swim. This works best when bodies are small enough to keep the tub relatively uncrowded, but the children are old enough to easily sit up safely. I got a lot of mileage out of this activity the winter my daughters were two and four. Of course, you should never, ever leave children unattended in the tub. Before allowing them in, grab the phone, a magazine, and anything else you think you might need at the "beach" so you don't need to run off once they're in the water. Then sit nearby, relax, and let the children splash.

EGG CARTON SORTING

Babies love to "put and take," and this is a simple way to entertain an older baby or toddler with items easily available. Grab an empty egg carton (hijack one from the fridge and put the eggs elsewhere, if need be!), then gather as many egg-sized toys or other safe objects as you can find around the house. They need not be round or oval-shaped, but they should fit into the cups of the carton. Examples include: small plastic or wooden alphabet blocks, rubber balls, miniature stuffed animals, finger puppets, dolly bottles, toy cars, and giant plastic "pop-on" beads. Be sure not to use any "chokeable" items or things you don't want your child to potentially suck on (if she's at that age). Place the filled egg carton in front of your child on the floor, then show her how to take the items out of the carton and put them back in. Help her count each space, one to twelve. Encourage her to move the objects around, sort by color or pattern, or, as she gets older, give her simple commands such as "Take out all but two of the toys" or "Can you put three things in the carton? Four? Five?"

This activity encourages counting, color, shape, and pattern recognition, and fine motor development. Kids love to see what sizes and shapes fit into the cups, move them around, even open and close the egg carton lid! Truly an example of simplicity in action.

CARS AND RAMPS

Kids of all ages love this activity. Gather all your small toy cars, trucks, and anything else with wheels. Make stacks of varying heights on the floor using large hardcover books—the bigger, the better. Then add a cookie sheet, sloping downward from the top of the book stack to the floor. Voila! A perfect ramp for sending cars and trucks down. Try experimenting with taller/steeper ramps vs. shorter/gentler slopes: which ramp sends the vehicles down farther and faster? Do large cars and trucks go faster than tiny Matchbox cars?

TOY CUPBOARD/DRAWER

One thing that will save you as a stay-at-home mom is having something to keep your baby/toddler busy in the kitchen while you cook. Your best bet is to find a bottom cupboard or low drawer that you can empty of household supplies and instead relegate to the baby. When my firstborn was a baby, we had a microwave cart that was perfect for this purpose. My husband removed the doors to the cupboard part of the cart (to prevent finger pinches), and we filled the Toy Cupboard with infant/toddler toys that Julia could pull out and play with over and over. (I rotated the toys occasionally to keep the contents interesting.) When we moved to a house with a larger kitchen and more cabinets and my second daughter was born, she got an entire double bottom cabinet as her Toy Cupboard. She'd sit on the floor and happily explore the contents of her cabinet while I attended to my own kitchen tasks, and it was a lifesaver!

Another option is to use a low, easy-to-open drawer, although be aware that little fingers can sometimes be pinched if a drawer rolls closed too easily.

In addition to baby toys, remember that cupboards and drawers can be filled with baby-safe kitchen items such as Tupperware containers, plastic bowls, wooden spoons, measuring cups, dish towels, and lightweight baking pans. Babies and toddlers love to "play cook!"

HOMEMADE SOFT PRETZELS

Sometimes you just gotta get down and dirty in the kitchen. When your kids are old enough to do some real cooking (so to speak), this is a great toddler/preschooler activity.

Recipe for Soft Pretzels

> 1 pkg. yeast
> ¾ c. warm water
> 1 T. sugar
> 2 c. flour
> ½ tsp. salt
> 1 egg for glazing
> Coarse salt for dusting

Preheat oven to 400 degrees. Line a baking sheet with foil, and then spray foil with nonstick cooking spray.

Sprinkle 1 package of yeast onto ¾ cup warm water in a small bowl. Add 1 T. sugar and stir. Let stand until mixture foams (about five minutes).

Put 2 cups flour and ½ tsp. salt in large bowl. Add the yeast mixture and stir.

Spread a handful of flour onto the counter or a large cutting board. Knead the dough until smooth.

Roll pieces of dough into ropes and make different shapes: circles, letters, spirals, etc. Kids especially love to make their initials!

Beat 1 egg with fork, then brush onto pretzels with a pastry brush. Sprinkle with salt (coarse is best, but any type will work).

Place on the cookie sheet and bake for 15 minutes or until light brown.

SHAVING CREAM "FINGER PAINTING"

Here's an even easier idea than using actual finger paint. All you need is a can of shaving cream and some baking sheets. Set your child up at the table or in a place where he or she can get messy. (As with actual paint, a table cover of some sort and a paint smock for your child are ideal.) Squirt some shaving cream onto a clean, dry baking sheet and let your child use his or her hands and fingers to draw, write, or just squish and play with the "finger paint." Easy, delightfully messy, and fun!

HOMEMADE PLAY DOUGH

Even if you have a lot of store-bought play dough in your house (as we do), making play dough at home is great fun, and it helps answer that favorite kids' winter-time (anytime?) refrain, *What should we do today?* True, the stovetop stirring is parents-only, and even the mixing is too hard for babies, but toddlers and preschoolers love to help where they can, and all ages can enjoy the playing after it has cooled. Just make sure the babes don't decide to eat it. (I admit, this is tough.)

RECIPE FOR HOMEMADE PLAY DOUGH

1 c. flour

½ c. salt

2 tsp. cream of tartar (find it in the spice aisle)

1 c. water

1 T. vegetable oil

Food coloring, scented extracts such as almond or peppermint

Combine flour, salt, and cream of tartar in a saucepan.

In a small bowl, combine water, oil, food coloring, and peppermint or

190

almond extract (optional).

Gradually stir wet ingredients into the dry ones in the saucepan until smooth.

Cook over medium heat, stirring constantly, until a ball forms.

Remove from stove. Cool before playing.

Store in an airtight container.

Recipe can be easily doubled, or repeated to make multiple colors.

HOMEMADE FINGER PAINT

For some reason, I put off making homemade finger paint for a long time—I guess because I feared it would be too difficult or complicated, or that one would need a special Homemade Finger Paint Talent Gene, which I wasn't sure I possessed.

Let me assure you, one does not. It is easy, and even if you screw up a little bit and overcook it as I did the first time I made it, ending up with an art material that is a bit on the....*gelatinous* side, it still works just fine and guess what? Small children don't even care. And they *love* stirring up the ingredients (the non-cooking parts, of course) and squeezing in the food coloring.

RECIPE FOR HOMEMADE FINGER PAINT

½ c. cornstarch

4 T. sugar

2 c. cold water

Food coloring

Mix ½ cup cornstarch and 4 T. sugar in a large pot.

Add 2 c. cold water and stir.

Cook mixture over medium heat, stirring constantly until it

*becomes thick. (Here is where things can become a bit chancy.
Strive for a non-runny, but still creamy, paint-like consistency.)*

Remove pot from heat and let cool.

*When cool, divide mixture into small plastic containers and add
food coloring.*

Use to finger-paint on paper, paper plates, or cookie sheets.
(Don't forget a vinyl "picnic-style" tablecloth or some taped-down
newspaper to protect the table and a paint smock or old oversized
t-shirt to protect your child's clothes.)

BUBBLY KITCHEN-SINK PLAY

This activity is for children old enough to stand safely on a
kitchen chair or stool, and tall enough to reach the sink while
doing so. It's great on cold winter days when warm water feels
especially good on chilly hands.

Fill the sink with water. Add dishwashing soap for bubbles.
(If you have a double sink, it's fun to fill one side with soapy water
and one side with just water.) Add measuring cups, funnels, and
large plastic spoons. Place an extra towel or two on the floor to
absorb splashes. Put a smock or apron on your child, stand him
or her up on the chair, and let her go to town. It doesn't get any
easier than this, but children never seem to tire of water play!

OUTDOOR ICE CUBE PLAY

Speaking of water play, here's a cool variation for easy,
outdoor, summertime fun. Keep your freezer stocked with plenty
of ice. On a hot day, empty a bunch of ice cubes into a plastic

toy bin (or whatever you have handy) and set it out on your patio, deck, driveway, or lawn. Let your child use big plastic cooking spoons to scoop the ice cubes in and out, "draw" with ice cubes on the pavement, experiment with feeling the cubes melt in her hands, and dunk them in and out of water buckets. Fun—and *cool*!

A variation on the above activity involves slightly more advance preparation but expands on the fun. Try freezing water in little containers, adding a bit of food coloring for fun, and letting the wee ones loose with that. This was a huge hit the summer my girls were toddlers. They were entranced by the frozen containers of green, yellow, and blue water (old Tupperware, measuring cups) I placed at their feet on the patio. To the mix, I added plastic buckets and spoons, and as the ice began to melt, they busied themselves stirring the colored water, dumping out the Tupperware-shaped, brilliantly-colored ice, and water-painting with the runoff. Sure, it's a bit messy, but they're outside, so who cares?!

WATER PAINTING

An oldie but goodie, this is another outdoor water-play activity that children seem to never tire of. All you need is a bucket or two of water (one per child is best) and some old paintbrushes (the kind you use to paint walls or furniture, not tiny ones for making art). When it's hot and your children are tired of the wading pool and running through the sprinkler, let them "paint" with water on pavement. My sisters and I grew up with this activity, and now my daughters spend many a summer day doing the same thing. Fun for many different ages!

OUTDOOR CAR WASH

Another hot-summer-day idea. Head out to the driveway with buckets of water (soapy and plain), and plenty of washrags and sponges. Have your child collect all his or her (non-wooden, water-safe) toy cars and trucks for an outdoor "car wash."

When the toys are clean, why not wash the "real" ride-on toys in the garage as well? Turn the car wash into a bicycle, tricycle, scooter, Big Wheel, and little-red-wagon wash, and let your child give the vehicles a good scrub!

DOLLY BATH

Even boy toddlers or preschoolers love playing "babies" now and then. One way to expand upon this imaginative play is to let your child give the dollies a bath in the tub or sink. Make sure the dolls in question are all-plastic and safe for the tub. Then run some lukewarm water (bubble bath is nice), find a washcloth or bath sponge, and tell your parent-in-training to give the babies a bath. Be sure to have towels handy for drying off afterwards! (Of course, you should never, ever leave children unattended in the tub.)

LEAF RUBBINGS

Surely you remember this classic autumn art project from your own childhood. Well, it's time to break it out! All you have to do is go on a walk to collect some nice fall leaves, bring them home and place them under a piece of paper, then rub an unwrapped crayon (lying down flat on the paper) over the paper to bring out the outlines of the leaves below. It looks best when you use an assortment of autumn-leaf colors, such as orange, red, yellow, and brown, but of course there's no reason your toddler's leaf rubbing couldn't be rendered in pink and purple.

NATURE COLLAGE

Remember when you collected leaves for leaf rubbings? Did you also think to collect all sorts of other fall nature specimens, like acorns, pine cones, twigs, flowers, berries, pebbles, bark, and seeds, in order to make an autumn nature collage? Kids love this project. Grab some paper plates and Elmer's glue, and show your kids how to glue their treasures from a morning's walk onto a plate (or two or three). Free-form art! And seasonal, too. (Obviously, you could do this in any season, depending on the weather and the natural foliage outside your door.)

SEED COLLECTION

The autumn my daughters were two and four, we began a seed collection. We went on a walk in our neighborhood, hunting for any type of seeds and placing them gently in a Ziploc bag to take home with us. Along the way, we had plenty of time to talk about what seeds are, what types we might find—acorns, pine cones (seeds inside), seed pods from leafy trees, fluffy white dandelion heads—and what grows from them. When we got home we transferred our treasures to the cups of an empty egg carton. We continued to add to the collection here and there; one day on a family walk, we found a milkweed pod and some green acorns. It was a fun science lesson to learn about seeds, and it was a great way to enjoy the lovely autumn days.

By expanding upon or limiting your hunt as needed, this activity works for a wide range of ages. Toddlers love to hold round, smooth acorns and explore their bumpy "hats"; a fourth-grader could research different types of seeds at the library (or, let's face it, on the Internet) and get really scientific about it.

Have fun on your own seed hunt!

APPLE PRINTING

Another kid classic, apple printing can turn ordinary painting into a novel, and therefore more toddler-engrossing, arts-and-crafts activity. Protect your table with an old tablecloth or vinyl cover, your child's clothes with a paint smock, and pour some (preferably washable) "poster"-type paint into a wide, shallow bowl, rimmed plate, or pie dish. (Separate dishes with different paint colors are nice.) Cut an apple in half (lengthwise or crosswise; they give different patterns), and remove seeds from holes. If you can, push a Popsicle stick into the back of the apple half (for easier handling); if you don't have any available, try sturdy toddler silverware or let your child just use his fingers to lift and maneuver the apple. It's more slippery and a bit tricky, but it will do.

Place the apple half cut-side down in the paint, rubbing it around a bit to make sure it's well coated. Lift, and press onto a sheet of paper, a paper plate, or a paper bag. Repeat to make various colors and designs. Note that other fruits and veggies are interesting for paint printing, too. Try stout carrots, bell peppers, or star fruit. Carve a design into a potato and print with that. Experiment with whatever's in your crisper drawer, fruit bowl, or pantry!

INDOOR OBSTACLE COURSE

When you're stuck inside but the kiddos are running wild, harness all that energy and set up an indoor obstacle course. It doesn't have to be complicated, and as a mom with two kids in a small basement-less townhome, I can tell you from experience that you don't need as much room as you might think. Just use your imagination to construct some "stations" for your kids to run through, decide on a starting line, model the course for them a time or two, then set them loose. Time them or not, make it a contest or don't, change up the course as needed. Just have fun! Some ideas for obstacle course stations and activities are:

- Run up/down the staircase
- Leap into a pile of pillows on the floor
- Hop through a hula hoop laid on the floor
- Toss beanbags or balls into a bucket, toy bin, or cooking pot
- Do 10 jumping jacks in a particular spot (say, on the welcome mat by the door)
- "Hurdle" over a belt, scarf, or jump-rope outstretched on the floor
- Do a somersault
- Crawl from one room to the next
- Have a "station" near the CD player for a minute or two of crazy dancing

Obviously, if you're lucky enough to own any indoor-active gear like a mini-trampoline, fold-up child's play tunnel, or giant fitness ball, incorporate those in your obstacle course. But the main idea is to just use what you have, keep it fun, and improvise as necessary. This is a great way for children to "get their wiggles out" when winter weather keeps you all inside.

INDOOR BOWLING

Another great winter activity, indoor bowling is best done in a long hallway. Set up stuffed animals as "pins." (If you happen to have empty plastic bottles to use as pins, even better, but kids often find it especially fun to topple plush bears and puppies.) Use any ball you can find as your bowling ball. Don't worry about pin formation or proper ball rolling technique. Just let the kids have at it.

FLOOR/WALL MURAL

Most children love to color and draw, and this project shakes things up a bit with giant paper and an unusual "easel." If you have access to a big roll of butcher paper or blank newsprint, great; otherwise, sacrifice some of your wrapping-paper (the kind that comes on large rolls) to the effort.

Tape an oversized stretch of paper, white side out, to a span of linoleum or other hard floor or to a large blank wall. Let your children create giant murals on the paper; they'll get a big kick out of the unconventional artwork. Who wouldn't?! It's like permission to color on the walls!

During the winter, white crayons or chalk on dark colored paper is especially fun, for creating snowmen and other snowy scenes.

PAPER PLATE MASKS

Here's a fun art project for preschoolers and up. You'll need plain white uncoated paper plates, crayons or markers, scissors, and yarn.

Take a paper plate and cut holes for eyes, a nose, and mouth. Have your child decorate the plate and/or draw around the holes with crayons or markers (i.e., add eyebrows, rosy cheeks, eyelashes, etc.). He or she can glue yarn scraps on the top for hair or the bottom for a beard, if desired. Punch holes on either side of the mask, then thread yarn through the holes to tie the mask around your child's head.

GIANT PASTA NECKLACES

You know those necklaces small children sometimes make in preschool, little dried noodles strung onto yarn? Sometimes decorated with paint or glitter? Well, that alone is a great idea, really—one of those old classics. But what if you, just for fun, used three-year-old manicotti noodles you forgot you had in your pantry, and made giant pasta necklaces? And painted them with Crayola washable easel paint? Wouldn't your kiddos love that? Go to it.

PAPER PLATE (OR CUP) SHAKERS

Another craft project for the preschool-and-older set, shakers require nothing more than paper plates or cups, crayons, markers, and/or stickers for decoration, dried beans, uncooked rice or pasta, or popcorn kernels for the inside, and masking or packaging tape to hold the pieces together.

Let your child decorate her plates or cups first. Then, pour some noisemaking material inside one of them. Place the second on top, and tape securely. For extra fun, make extras! Now she's ready to serenade you with her homemade "maracas"! Throw a parade, concert, or dance party with your new musical instrument.

GALLERY OF FACES

This one isn't so much an activity as it is a *strategy*. When my daughters were infants, I learned that they became entranced when confronted with large photos of faces—particularly faces of children or other babies. Parenting-magazine pages became my lifesaver, as I tore out and collected as many full-page photos of babies, toddlers, and children as I could find. Bright colors, close-ups, big smiles—all good. I taped them at baby-gazing height to the sides of my lower kitchen cabinets, the dishwasher door, and the dining-room wall, where I could sit the baby in her bouncy seat—or later, her ExerSaucer—in front of her "gallery of faces." These pages were up for months, and every guest to my house asked what they were for, and was intrigued and delighted by my explanation. My babies loved these pictures, and would sit and/or play happily near them for good stretches of time while I folded clothes or cooked. Brilliant!

Note: pages like this are also great for giving babies a "view" from their car seats. Tape securely to the back seat of your car, so your baby has something to look at it when riding rear-facing in her infant car seat. When she's big enough to turn around in her seat, she'll likely be happily distracted by her newfound forward view, but you can still tape magazine photo pages to the back of the front seats of your car for her to enjoy.

CARDBOARD BOX FUN

There's something heartwarming about the old-school activity of pretend-play with an empty box.

One fall day, when my girls were two and four, we discovered the book *Not A Box*, by Antoinette Portis, at the public library. It's a simple, clever, charming picture book about a line-drawn rabbit using his/her imagination to turn a large empty box into a race car, mountain peak, skyscraper, hot-air balloon, robot, rocket, etc. Inspired by this book, I rounded up some empty boxes (well, one box and one unused Rubbermaid storage bin), and Julia and Genevieve spent the morning climbing in and out their imaginary trains, tugboats, and school buses.

It was Julia's idea to actually act out the book page by page. The girls had me read it several times in a row so they could do it over and over again. Later, they piled stuffed animals and dolls into their boxes and gave rides to all the babies and creatures. Fun for all—and for hours.

BABY STORYTIME

I know that storytime doesn't exactly seem brilliantly original, right? Who doesn't read stories to their kids? Allow me to elaborate.

In both places my family has lived since my first daughter was born, there have been great free "Baby Storytimes" in town; first, at a well-known children's bookshop in St. Paul, and now, at our town's public library. The St. Paul bookshop was my gold standard; its storytime session included not just stories (by a very talented children's singer and storyteller), but also puppets, singing, finger games, rhymes, musical instruments, and even acknowledgment of the first birthdays of any babies in attendance who happened to be celebrating such a milestone that particular week. As you might expect, this storytime was a huge hit, known far and wide amongst parents across the city, and always jam-packed. Our current local library's storytime is a far less extravagant offering, but it's still fun, social, and great enrichment for my younger daughter, and Julia before her.

When Julia was a toddler and Genevieve just a year old, I used to bring both of them to the library's baby storytime, because older siblings are always welcome, and Julia loved "helping" the babies and following along. Thus, we started a little home version of baby storytime at some point (sometimes referred to by Julia, sweetly, as "Songs and Stories With Genevieve"). Mimicking the best of our storytime experiences, we included plenty of songs, nursery rhymes, musical instrument playing, and action games like "Ring Around the Rosie," interspersed amongst a selection of baby board books and longer stories.

On our best days, Baby Storytime could run a good 20 minutes. Who knows, maybe you can get a whole half hour out of it! You could even choose a theme for each time, picking books and songs that converge on one idea: seasons? flowers? farm animals?

Good luck, and may the force of the best children's librarians everywhere be with you.

DOLL/TEDDY BEAR TEA PARTY (INDOORS OR OUT)

Toddlers, preschoolers, and kindergartners love to engage in pretend play, using their imaginations to mimic caretaking behavior with dolls and stuffed animals. One sweet way to harness this creativity and keep them busy at the same time is to encourage them to host a dolly or bear tea party. This can take place indoors, at a child-sized table or on the floor, or outdoors on the lawn as a tea party picnic.

If you happen to have a toy tea set to use, great; but unbreakable toddler dishes work fine too. Let your child serve water as pretend "tea," and either plastic play "food" for refreshments or perhaps a real graham cracker or two. Very sweet!

DRESSER DRAWER/SORTING CLOTHES

There's a certain age of baby-/toddlerhood when wee ones love nothing more than to sit on the floor in front of an open bottom dresser drawer, repeatedly pulling each item of clothing out onto the floor and then stuffing them back in. When my firstborn daughter Julia was around one, she would do this endlessly, with utter concentration and bottomless glee. Needless to say, I gladly took advantage of this stage, and frequently placed her in front of an open clothes drawer so I could get a few things done around the house—or just rest for a moment! Sure, eventually I'd have a big heap of baby clothes to refold and put away neatly, but that was a very fair price to pay!

When children get a little older, they still like this "game," only now you can actually put them to work. At the turn of the seasons, I like to instruct my kindergartner, Genevieve, to help me switch out my daughters' wardrobes by culling all the clothing items to be stored or given away ("Find all the tank tops and sleeveless shirts for me, honey, and make a big pile," or "Pull out any winter sweaters."). This makes my job a bit easier, but more importantly, it makes my child happy and keeps her occupied while I actually complete a task that needs doing.

HOUSEHOLD CHORE HELPER

I can't stress enough the brilliance of having your young child do your chores, housework, and cooking tasks with you. *They love this!* When Julia was in kindergarten every morning, and Genevieve was home with me, we did this all the time.

Of course the key is presenting these activities in such a way as to make them seem Extremely Exciting and Helpful, and things that only Big, Important Children Can Do. A peppy, gleeful tone of voice is a prerequisite. Interestingly, pinning the idea on *another* mom that the child knows and loves seems to work especially well: "Do you know what great idea *Lucy's mom* does with her girls sometimes? It's *so* cool." And then you describe something totally mundane that you need to get done anyway, like dusting the furniture.

Genevieve loves to help me dust. I give her a damp rag and tell her she's in charge of dusting her toys and anything low and I can get the whole house done this way. Sweeping or dust-mopping the floor is good too.

Small children are not especially good at actually cleaning, but if they can happily do their own version of whatever chore you need to get done, you can cross it off your to-do list and know that your kid has had fun, too. I give Genevieve our Swiffer (which is broken, so the handle is conveniently short and just her size), and I use the broom at the same time. She's just having fun, but I'm actually cleaning the floor.

It's amazing how much joy and interest small children can get out of simple household tasks. Sure, sometimes you'll be busy reading books, going for walks, and doing art projects with them. And sometimes you can set them up with an activity to do on their own, while you sip coffee and read the newspaper oops I mean wash the dishes and do the laundry, but sometimes you just need to get things done, and you also need to entertain your kid, and guess what? That can be the same thing more often than you might think.

PLEASE
JOIN MY TRIBE

VISIT ME AT

WWW.SHANNONTASSAVA.COM

FOR MORE SELF-CARE RESOURCES AND UPDATES

Acknowledgments

Heartfelt thanks:

To Lori Culwell, who believed in this book when it was only a tiny idea in the back of my sleep-deprived mind, and then did everything she could possibly do to help make it a reality. I could never name all the things she has done for me.

To my dream editor Jane Slade, who understood my vision and my voice from the very beginning and made this book a better version of itself.

To Rita Arens and Arielle Eckstut for invaluable help with the proposal.

To Kristin Vickers Douglas, PhD, and Sheela Raja, PhD, fellow psychologists and beloved long-time friends, who supported the message of and need for this book.

To my online tribe of encouragers and supporters, none of whom I've met in real life but all of whom have cheered me on from afar and made my mothering life better. I love you for that. I trust you know who you are.

To my family and dearest friends, who came along on this ride and put up with an awful lot of talk about writing, motherhood, and lack of sleep.

To my husband Christopher, who's always there for me; and to Julia and Genevieve, whose title suggestions for this book were *You Get Better Homes with Babies* and *Happy Mom*, respectively.

And to all the other mamas out there who know just how life-changing and wonderful it is to be a mom, even during the hard parts.

Made in the USA
Lexington, KY
15 May 2012